If Jesus Were A Sportswriter

Parables From Sports

Charles J. Dobbins

1999

SEE: PHILIPPIANS 1:2

Charles J. Dobbins

ISBN 0-7414-0313-7

Published by:

Buy Books on the web.com
862 West Lancaster Avenue
Bryn Mawr, PA 19010-3222
Info@buybooksontheweb.com
www.buybooksontheweb.com
Toll-free (877) BUY BOOK

Printed in the United States of America

Printed on Recycled Paper

Published October-1999

This book is dedicated to three institutions:

(1) The Church - where three generations of Episcopal priests preceded me in the ministry, where Mother and Dad served faithfully and by their love taught me the love of God, where the congregation of Christ Church nurtured me. I am also indebted to the other Texas congregations who enriched and nourished my faith: Trinity, Port Neches, Epiphany, Houston, and Good Shepherd, Corpus Christi.

(2) Sports - especially to the Temple Wildcats of Temple, Texas, who began my love affair with sports and taught me the depth of devotion.

(3) Marriage - for my wife, Anne, who put forth great love and devotion to be able to share knowingly and completely in my two other loves.

FOREWORD

I decided to make creative use of the words of editors who rejected this book. That also could be a parable.

These are, naturally, the best comments:

"We do appreciate and thank you for sending us: IF JESUS WERE A SPORTSWRITER, a purposeful, and well-written, non-fiction manuscript which edifies the will to pursue a victorious Christian life. It is broad and striking and we are sure that this volume will not only enrich others who read it, but also you, the spiritual author."

". . . I like many of your parables. I especially like your idea of using Theophilus as a storyteller. And I think that your terse quotations of Scripture at the end are 'right on.' . . ."

"Many thanks for sending us your sample parables based on sports. . . . Your idea is clever and your writing style is quite readable, appealing to a broad audience."

PREFACE

As I wrote this book, I had to decide upon a name. When I got the idea, I realized that some might think it is shocking that I could conceive of Jesus as a sportswriter. However, this is no more amazing than the idea that the Messiah could be a carpenter (Mark 6:3a).

My hope for this book is that you will question the meaning that I give to each parable and give another meaning based on your experiences. The desired result of this effort is to connect your interest in sports with your interest in Christ. I also urge you to read the Biblical quotations in their scriptural context and relate those messages with the parables in this book.

The Greek meaning of the word "parable" is "side by side." This book combines stories from sports and Jesus' parabolic teaching method to add a new dimension to your understanding of the Christian faith.

When Jesus was born, the great truths were passed from generation to generation by stories. When these stories were given a spiritual meaning, they were called parables. Jesus undoubtedly learned parables from his rabbis. He also learned stories from his parents, the men who sat around the carpenter's shop, and his own experiences. Some were lengthy and some were one-liners. Jesus told these stories and then applied them to the God-man relationship and they became parables. Their meaning receives authority from the author.

This book is the meaning that I give to the parables, and therefore it lacks authority. However, even in the Scriptures, parables can have different uses depending on when and why they were told. The parable of the sower was told by Jesus to his followers to warn them that everyone won't respond. The Gospel of Mark attaches a sermon to it (Mark 4:13-20) to include those who have no roots because of the persecutions. Similarly, the parable of the ten virgins is used by Jesus to indicate that many were unprepared for the coming of the Messiah. The early church used it to prepare for the Second Coming. "Watch out, then, because you do not know the day or the hour" (Matthew 25:13). Since the first or second comings are not my concern here, I used it for being prepared when opportunity comes. I trust that all three are Christian in their meaning.

The stories from sports come from many different sources: sportswriters, athletes, and my own athletic endeavor. I take stories and I place them side-by-side with my own understanding that I bring to each story.

Notes on these Parables

(1)   Theophilus - The person to whom Luke addressed his Gospel and the Book of Acts. His name means "Friend of God," and thus he was chosen to narrate parables from my personal experiences or ideas.

(2)   Personal Names - Following the example of Scripture, proper names are not used in the parables.

Charles J. Dobbins
Rockport, Texas

CONTENTS

❃

THE PARABLES OF BASEBALL

The Tweener 3
Nothing Lasts 4
The Sacrifice 5
The Loving Owner 6
The Baseball Diamond 7
The Shot Heard Round the World 8
Many Attend 9
Tinker to Evers to Chance 10
The No-Hitter 11
A Banquet 12
Keeping Score 13
The Luckiest Man 14
A Blue Chipper 15

❃

THE PARABLES OF BASKETBALL

Season Tickets 19
The Charity Line 20
The Coach 21
The Star 22
The Missed Free Throws 23
Nobody Roots for Goliath 24
Seeing a Game 25

THE PARABLES OF BOXING

The Bee and the Bomber	29
The Big Cat	30
The Big Fight	31
A Tragic Death	32
The Size of the Dog	33
The Left Jab	34
One-Eyed Connelly	35

THE PARABLES OF FOOTBALL

The Blocked Punt	39
First Downs	40
The Red Zone	41
The Unprepared	42
The Talents	43
Spontaneity	44
Both	45
The Member	46
The Unjust School Board	47
The Gipper	48
Tradition	49
The Turnover	50
Ten Days in August	51
The Line Coach	52
A Record of 7-3	53
Putting On	54
The Diagram	55

Statistics   56
Half Lose   57
The 12th Man   58
Ties   59
Luck   60
The Dance   61

✂

THE PARABLES OF GOLF

The Lost Golf Ball   65
The Putter   66
The 8-Iron   67
The Mulligan   68
The Handicap   69
The Cleanest Game   70
The Bad Lie   71

✂

THE PARABLES OF
HUNTING – FISHING – SAILING

Old Tip   75
The Cat's Paw   76
Against the Wind   77
Crabbing   78
The Steeplechase   79

�֎

THE PARABLES OF MOST SPORTS

The Rules Committee   83
Jimmy the Greek   84
"Old Mo"   85
Free Agency   86
Sin   87
The Three Bones   88
The Kingdom   89
The Defense   90
Believing   91
The Natural   92
Wait Till Next Year   93

✖

THE PARABLES OF RACING

Fixing a Race   97
The Pits   98
An Eight Year Old   99
A Goat   100
The Leader   101
The High Bar   102
The Man Against the Horse   103
The First Day   104
Charismata   105

�֎

THE PARABLES OF SOCCER AND HOCKEY

On Simplicity	109
Pre-Match Ritual	110
Angles	111
A National Team	112
The Big Goal	113
Absolute Joy	114
No Stats	115

✖

THE PARABLES OF TENNIS & VOLLEYBALL

The Love Game	119
The Linesman	120
Serving	121
The Tournament	122
Sight and Sound	123
A Name	124
A Game Plan	125

✖

AMEN

Amen Corner	129

✖

Divider Quotations	131

BASEBALL

*"Next to religion, baseball has had a greater impact
on the American people
than any other institution."*

Herbert Hoover, 35th President of the United States

The Parable of the Tweener

A certain coach[1] was umpiring a baseball game. The home team led by one run in the ninth inning. The visitors had the bases loaded with two outs and a full count on the batter. The pitch crossed the plate and the umpire said, "Tweener!" Both sides rushed to the umpire with the same question: "What's a tweener?" The umpire replied, "It is when a pitch is too low to be a strike and too high to be a ball."

The closest thing to a "tweener" in sports was instant replay in professional football. This allowed referees in the press box to review close calls by looking at many television camera shots. Looking at things from different angles was a good idea, but the problem was that the decision also had to be instant, and the plan was dropped.

A "tweener" is like trying to make a decision between two choices and neither seems quite right. We are often told to do something even if it is wrong. The umpire in our parable decides to put off a decision and take another look. This is a difficult concept to convey - that doing nothing is doing something. If you can't decide, don't! The situation could change, then you don't have to decide. However, if you do, call it like you see it.

Philippians 1:23-24 - I am pulled in two directions. I want very much to leave this life and be with Christ, which is a far better thing; but for your sake it is much more important that I remain alive.

---

[1] Gordon M. Clark, Athletic Director of The University of the South, Sewanee, Tennessee.

3

The Parable of Nothing Lasts

This is the story of a pitcher who returned to his team's dugout and said, "I was good, eh?" His manager replied, "Your fastball was up and your curveball was hanging. In the majors, they would have ripped you." The pitcher replied, "Can't you let me enjoy the moment?" The manager said, "The moment is over."

The manager has learned the essential lesson of life. "Nothing lasts. The past is past. Everything must be achieved anew - on the next pitch, the next at bat, in the next game, the next season."[2]

Many times a person becomes a Christian because of one great moment in his life and witnesses to that moment over and over again. Any conversion type experience is remarkable, but the moment is over. In his writings, St. Paul never described his Damascus Road conversion because what was important was not his conversion experience but what it meant. His writings dealt with applying Christian principles to the specific problems in the early Church. They enable us to do the same. Christianity is a living faith and needs a witness to what the moment requires. We can only hope that what we have done will be fruit and bear seed.[3]

II Corinthians 10:18 - For it is when the Lord thinks well of a person that he is really approved, and not when he thinks well of himself.

---

[2] George F. Will, *Men At Work* (New York: Harper Perennial, 1990), 327.

[3] Werner and Lotte Pelz, *God is No More* (London: Victor Gallanez Ltd., 1963), 65.

The Parable of the Sacrifice

A third base coach was giving an assortment of signs and the runner was taking his lead away from first. The batter laid a bunt down the third base line and the runner was thrown out. The official ruled the play a sacrifice.

In baseball every bunt in this situation is not a sacrifice. The official scorer must decide if the batter is trying for a hit or attempting to move his teammate into scoring position. (That's a sacrifice.) It's not much of a sacrifice because it doesn't count as a time at bat.

Historically, sacrifice began with people sacrificing other people; Abraham offered Isaac.[4] It then moved to animals because animals were sinless and therefore more perfect than people. This continued until the perfect man was sacrificed, which was "a full, perfect, and sufficient sacrifice, oblation, and satisfaction, for the sins of the whole world."[5]

In all the types of sacrifice, the basic goal is to help a person or a people be in a position to score, get an education, win a war. Behind advancement there is usually a sacrifice. So while a sacrifice bunt is not like the Cross, the Cross is like a sacrifice bunt. Wherever a person discovers this, it will always be a Good Friday.

I John 3:16 - This is how we know what love is: Christ gave his life for us. We, too, then ought to give our lives for our brothers!

---

[4] Genesis 22.

[5] *The Book of Common Prayer* (Greenwich, CT: The Church Hymnal Corp. and Seabury Press, 1977), 334.

The Parable of the Loving Owner

A certain owner had two outfielders. One was a veteran and the other was a young star. The young star said to his owner, "Give me a break, release me from my contract so I can go to a big city and make big bucks." So the owner agreed, and the young star went to the big city. He spent his bigger contract with his new friends, on expensive clothes, restaurants, parties, and drugs. He was living high on the hog until he was suspended by the league for violating the drug code. He went back to his original owner to see if he could be a handyman around the stadium. But the owner said, "Stay off drugs, stay in shape, and when your suspension ends I'll put you back on the team." The owner was happy to have him back, but the faithful veteran was unhappy because he thought the owner had never done anything nice for him.

With its biblical base, my story should be called the parable of the prodigal player. However, the original form should never have been called The Parable of the Prodigal Son, for the son is not the hero. It should be called the Parable of the Loving Father, for it tells us rather about a father's love than a son's sin. It tells us much about the forgiveness of God.[6]

Forgiveness is never earned and is about the future and not the past.

Luke 15:11-32 - The Parable of the Prodigal Son

---

[6] William Barkley, *The Gospel of Luke* (Philadelphia: The Westminster Press, 1975), 205.

The Allegory of a Baseball Diamond

A teenager asked, "Why do they call me a southpaw?" His manager said, "Because they laid out baseball fields with the batter facing east so the afternoon sun was behind him. The pitcher faces west and the left arm is on the south side, so you're a southpaw."[7]

When possible, churches were built with the congregation facing east, which lends itself to an allegory. The baseball diamond is a church building. God has written the rules and he keeps statistics. The choir, ushers, and acolytes are the team, the preacher is the pitcher who controls the game, and the congregation represents the spectators.

But "Soren Kierkegard once made the observation that most of us have a mistaken notion about what a sermon is. We think of it as a play written by God, acted by a preacher, and observed by the congregation. On the contrary, he insisted, it is much more: the preacher is the playwright, the congregation is the company of actors, and God is the audience."[8]

So it turns out that the baseball diamond is still the church building. The preacher is the manager who directs the team, the congregation is the team, and God is the spectator. This allegory should help us understand that Christianity is not a spectator sport.

James 1:22 - Do not deceive yourselves by just listening to his word; instead, put it into practice.

---

[7] *Why Do We Say It?* (Edison, NJ: Castle Books, 1985), 226.
[8] C. FitzSimons Allison, *Fear, Love and Worship* (Greenwich, CT: The Seabury Press, 1962), 7.

The Parable of the Shot Heard Round the World

A certain sportswriter wrote this about a dramatic ending to a baseball game. "Now it is done. Now the story ends. And there is no way to tell it. The art of fiction is dead. Reality has strangled invention. Only the utterly impossible, the inexpressibly fantastic can ever be plausible again."[9]

Bobby Thompson's home run, like any dramatic ending to a sporting event, brings forth the greatest reactions. For the losers, it is the end of the world. For the winners, it is the second coming.

In Christian theology the dramatic ending is called Eschatology, which is concerned with the end of the history of the Earth and the ultimate hope for individuals and mankind.

"This idea contains the truth that God's eternal Kingdom shall not be only the end, but also the fulfillment and completion of our history with all its toil and struggle."[10]

The description of a dramatic ninth inning home run is a great description of the end of history. "Now it is done. Now the story ends." The end of the earth will actually be a run home.

I Corinthians 7:31 - For this world, as it is now, will not last much longer.

---

[9] Daniel Okrent and Steve Wolf, *Baseball Anecdotes* (New York: Oxford University Press, 1989), 223.
[10] Paul Athans, *Handbook of Christian Theology* (New York: Meridian Books, Inc., 1958), 105.

The Parable of Many Attend

"Catchers, who have the game in front of them and are in on every pitch, not only work harder than other everyday players, they are required to think more. It was naturally a catcher who said that baseball is like church: Many attend but few understand."[11]

Theology is the most exciting subject in the world, but like all learning we need every resource we can get. You can't be a Christian alone, and you can't learn about God alone. Like all fields of endeavor, the more we know the more we want to know, though some are content with a kindergarten understanding.

The greatest of all fears is the fear of the unknown (Angst). It causes us to be afraid that we will discover something that we don't like or don't believe. I believe it was Will Rogers who said, "Some people worry about the parts of the Bible they don't understand. I worry about the parts I do understand."

A famous referee talking about sports said, "The more you understand the rules and strategies of the game, the more you enjoy watching someone else handle the process of deciding what to do as the situation changes. Knowledge builds appreciation."[12] This is also true of your faith.

Philippians 1:9 - I pray your love will keep on growing more and more, together with true knowledge and perfect judgement.

---

[11] George F. Will, *Men At Work* (New York: Harper Perennial, 1990), 4.
[12] Jim Tunney, *Impartial Judgement* (Franklin Watts, 1988), XVII.

The Parable of Tinker to Evers to Chance

A certain sportswriter covered a game in which he saw the double play combination of the Chicago Cubs. He began his story with these words:

These are the saddest of possible words,
"Tinker to Evers to Chance."
Trio of Cubs, and fleeter than birds.
"Tinker to Evers to Chance."[13]

I believed that Tinker to Evers to Chance was the greatest double play combination. They were inducted into Baseball's Hall of Fame in 1936. Sportswriter Charlie Segar determined that from 1906 to 1909 the three men combined for only 56 double plays scored 4-6-3 or 6-4-3.[14]

Their reputation and induction as a combination into the Hall of Fame could be completely justified. It is impossible to compare baseball statistics in the different decades. However, it would appear that except for Frank Chance those players did not have numbers that were up to Hall of Fame standards. Your reputation can open many doors, but "Be more concerned with your character than with your reputation, because your character is what you really are, while your reputation is merely what others think you are."[15]

Ecclesiasticus 44:7 - All these men were honored in their generation and were the glory of their time.

---

[13] Lee Green, *Sportswit* (New York: Harper and Row, 1984), 61-62.
[14] Daniel Okrent and Steve Wolf, *Baseball Anecdotes* (New York: Oxford University Press, 1989), 51-52.
[15] Lee Green, *Sportswit* (New York: Harper and Row, 1984), 72. Quote by John Wooden, U.C.L.A. basketball coach.

The Parable of the No-Hitter

A baseball scout called the major league manager of his team and shouted, "I've landed the greatest young pitcher in the land. He struck out every man who came to bat - twenty-seven in a row. Nobody even got a foul until two were out in the ninth. The pitcher is right here with me. What shall I do?" The manager said, "Sign up the guy who got the foul. We're looking for hitters."[16]

The scout was doing his daily job of looking for good baseball players, and he found a great one, but the manager[17] was interested in someone else. This is very often the truth for those who are constantly seeking a great gem. I found one the day it occurred to me that one purpose of prayer is to help me see things from God's perspective, not to help God see things from mine. With great joy I shared my revelation with a friend; he wasn't interested at all and told me he was looking for something else.

Don't be disappointed because someday, somewhere, another person will be looking for what you have found and will share your joy. The Kingdom is like that.

Matthew 13:45-46 - Also, the Kingdom of Heaven is like this. A man is looking for fine pearls, and when he finds one that is unusually fine, he goes and sells everything he has, and buys that pearl.

---

[16] Clifton Fadiman, *The Little Brown Book of Anecdotes* (Boston: Little, Brown and Company, 1985), Grimm 1.
[17] The manager is Charlie Grimm.

The Parable of a Banquet

A certain baseball team was invited to a banquet by an automobile company. All of the players and the manager were invited, but only six came. Eighteen players and the manager didn't come. One said, "I never attend if I can possibly miss." One said, "My cousin came to town." The manager said, "I wouldn't go to that banquet if the Pope invited me." At the banquet, the emcee said, "We are going to present each of you who came tonight with a brand new 1936 Chevrolet."[18]

Banquets come in many forms, but they have two things in common. All are preceded by an invitation and an argument in the family over whether we have to go. Then the day arrives and we are reminded that this is the night of the banquet.

Most of us, like the ball players, try to make up a good excuse because there is not much joy in getting dressed-up and going to a large seated banquet.

In our parable, the six who did come experienced the joy that Christians expect when they come to the Messianic banquet.

Luke 14:15-24 – The Parable of the Great Supper

---

[18] Ernie Harwell, *Ernie Harwell's Diamond Gems* (Ann Arbor: Momentum Books, Ltd., 1991), 139-140.

The Parable of Keeping Score

Many years ago when a certain man and his future wife started dating and deciding where to go, the considerate man would say, "Let's go to the King Cole Room." The future wife, who disliked baseball, would nevertheless suggest that they go to see the Washington Senators play. When the Senators were in town she usually won the argument. And then the man taught his fiancée to keep score in the program, and this simple act opened a door that made her as avid a fan as her husband.

"You cannot announce baseball, you cannot write baseball, you cannot report baseball in any fashion unless you score it. Nor do I believe a fan can fully enjoy the game he sees unless he scores it in some fashion."[19]

Scoring helped her to understand the game, she became more aware of the situations and the answers. Who's covering second with a runner on first. Why a batter was walked. Who's coming to bat in the last inning. Knowing what caused you to win or lose makes you a better fan.

Some things need to be forgotten, but some need to be remembered. One of my favorite prayers is "Lord, help us to remember what we ought not to forget, and to forget what we ought not to remember."[20]

I Corinthians 13:5b - . . . love does not keep a record of wrongs.

---

[19] Red Barber, *The Broadcasters* (The Dial Press, 1970), 254.
[20] Robert N. Rodenmayer, *A Pastor's Prayerbook*, (New York: Oxford University Press, 1965), 262.

Parable of the Luckiest Man

In 1935, when a certain first baseman said: "Fans, for the past two weeks you have been reading about a bad break I got. Yet today I consider myself the luckiest man on the face of the earth. I have been in ballparks for seventeen years and I have never received anything but kindness and encouragement from you fans. Look at these grand men. Which of you wouldn't consider it the highlight of his career just to associate with them for even one day? Sure, I'm lucky. When you have a father and mother who work all their lives so that you can have an education and build your body, it's a blessing. When you have a wife who has been a tower of strength and shown more courage than you dream existed, that's the finest I know. So I close in saying that I might have had a bad break, but I have an awful lot to live for. Thank you."[21]

I included as much as possible of Lou Gehrig's speech because most things are better understood in the context of the whole. The "luckiest man" is said in spite of a horrible, fatal illness that will one day bear his name. The speech counts his blessings. I have often been asked by those with an illness, "What did I do to deserve this?" I've never been asked, "What did I do to deserve to be well?"

The luckiest people aren't those who avoid a bad break but those who see the many good breaks that make them lucky.

Romans 12:12 – Let your hope keep you joyful, be patient in your troubles, and pray at all times.

---

[21] Ray Robinson, *The Iron Horse* (New York: W. A. Norton and Co., 1990), 263-264.

The Allegory of a Blue Chipper

A Blue Chip prospect visits a college campus to interview and be interviewed. He returns home and his friends ask, "What was the program really like?"

His description begins with the coach because he is the one who creates, develops, and sustains the program.

Next he meets the players and each in his own way tells him what the coach and the program are really like.

Then that night he goes to a reception and talks to students, teachers, and alumni and he feels that indescribable something called school spirit, which includes the whole attitude of the school, the history, the lore, the great players who have passed the tradition on to this very moment.

When the early Christians were recruited and signed the letters of intent (another name for baptism), they were also asked to put into words what "Christian" was and what God was really like.

They had learned of God in three distinct ways but they knew there was only one God. The only way to explain these different aspects of the same program and keep the unity was to call it Tri-unity.

This trinity is necessary to describe a college program to a friend, and also necessary for Christians in describing their God.

Matthew 28:19 - Go, then, to all peoples everywhere and make them my disciples: Baptize them in the name of the Father, the Son and the Holy Spirit.

BASKETBALL

"When a game is on Ash Wednesday, and the ref shows up with a smudge on his forehead, I know I'm in trouble."

Jack McClosky, Wake Forest Basketball Coach
losing to St. Joseph

The Parable of the Season Tickets

A certain man and his wife decided to buy season tickets for the home games of a college basketball team. Following the decision the team's home schedule was placed on their personal appointment calendars. As plans were made, every meeting, every business obligation, every social invitation had to first clear the basketball schedule. The couple did not miss a single home game.

This parable is about the commitment that follows currency in a monetary society. It means that in all areas of life, if we put our money where our mouth is, then that activity will take on a richness. If a person has money invested in the stock market, he reads the business section of a newspaper. If a person has no stock but a season ticket, it means turning to the sports page.

Needless to say, money has many legitimate uses, one of which is pleasure. Sin begins, and begins only when passion replaces reason and rash intemperance induces suffering among others.[1] Having a good time is part of Christian living. The man and woman shouldn't buy season tickets if that interferes with Christian responsibilities to church, home, and society, but recreation is part of God's gift of re-creation for the souls of all.

Luke 12:34 - For your heart will always be where your riches are.

---

[1] Chad Walch and Eric Montizambert, *Faith and Behavior* (New York: Morehouse-Gordon Co., 1954), 28.

The Parable of the Charity Line

And he said unto them, "I was rebounding and you came over my back; I was defending and you used a running pick; I was taking a shot and you hacked me; I was running out the clock and you grabbed me." And you said, "When did I come over your back, or pick you or hack you, or grab you?" But the referees saw your wrongdoing and sent me to the charity line.

Many people believe that a charity line is getting something for nothing. However, a person goes to the charity line after a foul has been committed. Sometimes the fouls are technical, but most are personal. Each in its own way is hindering someone in the pursuit of a goal.

Some people in life, who are sent to the charity line, come there because they are unable to rebound when they are held down by health, hardship or education. Some are sent because their employer picks a new location and they are unable to move. Some go because they just can't hack it. Some are sent to the charity line because their time is running out.

The question this parable asks of each of us is, "Do you only see the other side's fouls?"

See: Matthew 25:31-46 - The Parable of Sheep and Goats

The Parable of the Coach

A certain professional basketball coach[2] explained why he had trouble applying the Golden Rule to his players: "I tried to treat them like me and some of them weren't."[3]

The trouble with the Golden Rule is that it uses yourself as the standard. There are other considerations outside yourself that form the basis of what is "good".

Bill Russell when he was a player wanted his coach to demand discipline, 100% effort, and team players. It is rather obvious that many players who get to the N.B.A. on talent don't want to be treated the way Bill Russell wanted to be treated.

On a different level, if I believe that I should be kicked by my teammates when I miss a free throw, then when my teammate misses a free throw I should kick him.

Thus, the Golden Rule works when you and I have the same standard - ("I tried to treat them like me"). However, for Christians, Jesus is the best standard for our actions. It is a far better standard to treat people as you believe Jesus would than to treat others as you would want them to treat you.

Matthew 7:12a - Do for others what you want them to do for you.

---

[2] Bill Russell.

[3] Andrew J. Maikovich, *Sports Quotations* (Jefferson, NC: McFarland and Company, Inc., 1984), 594.

The Parable of the Star

There was a college basketball star who after graduation had to begin his professional career in the Continental League. Each year, different N.B.A. teams brought him up as a replacement player, but he was always cut and returned to the Continental League, where he was a star. One year he was leading the league in rebounds near the end of the season, when a power forward on a contending N.B.A. team was injured and sidelined for the remainder of the season. The star was selected to replace the injured player, he helped the team to win the championship of the N.B.A., and he got the ring so many desire to win.

The parable of Jesus listed below encourages us to persist in prayer, to resolutely pursue our goal.

· The sports parable is but one of many examples of players who never gave up until they got what they wanted, with the same importunity as the bothersome widow.

In the Christian life one of the easiest things to do is to quit praying. Our concerns change very little and therefore our prayers are repetitious. Our prayers must always go beyond the limit of our sight.

See: Parable of the Unjust Judge. Luke 18:1-8

The Parable of the Missed Free Throws

The point guard was an 87% free throw shooter and stood at the foul line with two free shots. His team was behind by one point with two seconds left to play. The minimum he needed to do was to tie the game, and two free throws would win it. The first bounced around on the rim and fell off. The second hit the backboard and bounced into the hands of the opponents' center. The radio announcer said, "Oh, no, he lost the game! We're eliminated from the tournament!"

The disappointment of the moment caused the announcer to commit a heresy. I call it a heresy because teams lose games. Every player on the losing team missed a shot that could have won the game. Every player either missed a rebound, committed a turn-over, committed a foul, or missed a free throw that could have won the game. But sharing the guilt doesn't help, I missed the shot.

So we turn it into something good. I'll be a better player because I'll work harder. The team will be better next year and this elimination will motivate us. But that only soothes my guilt.

The truth is that the "if onlys" would not necessarily end happily. In the flights of imagination about the glories of what might have been, the simplest check is the repetition to oneself of four other little words: "How do I know?"

Philippians 3:13b - . . .the one thing I do, however, is to forget what is behind me and do my best to reach what is ahead.

Nobody Roots for Goliath

Theophilus told another parable: a certain professional baseball center[4] said, "Nobody roots for Goliath."

The question to be answered by the parable that nobody roots for Goliath is: Are we against Goliath or for David? We admire those with less prowess who overcome the odds to achieve a goal. At the same time, when the top ranked person loses because he failed to use his obvious superiority, we dislike the misuse of talent.

It is rather obvious that all people are not physically created equal. Not everyone can be an N.B.A. center. However, some of the greatest sports stories are the athletes who work constantly at being better, the athletes who give an all-out effort at every opportunity. Equally true is that when the natural superstar works hard to improve each year and becomes a star like Michael Jordan, we do cheer for a giant.

God does not call us to be Goliath or David, only ourselves. He does ask us when we reach one level of achievement to raise our goal to a higher level and, as we grow older and our talents wane, to invest our experience and make different types of contributions. As someone has said, "The greatest enemy of the best is the good."

Romans 12:6a - So we are to use our different gifts in accordance with the grace that God has given us.

---

[4] Wilt Chamberlain, *New York Times*, November 17, 1978.

The Parable of Seeing the Game

A boy always had to settle for second string position. Yet his father never missed a game. After his father's death the son, with tears in his eyes, said "Coach, please let me start tonight. I want to play for Dad."

The boy played a phenomenal game and the Coach asked him how he accomplished it. The son said, "Coach, I played that one for Dad. My father never missed a game, but he never saw me play - until tonight! You see, Coach, my father was blind."[5]

Many of us have experienced the joy of rising to the occasion and performing beyond our capabilities. I have done this in an important game. It's called coming through in the clutch. I have done this in crucial sermons when the message of God had to be communicated through my words. I have done this when the right thing was said at the right time to resolve a difficult problem.

It is in these moments that we feel the presence of God in our talents, words, and deeds. The more we feel God's watchful eye the more we will see him not only in the extraordinary but in the ordinary.

Luke 10:23 - Then Jesus turned to the disciples and said to them privately, "How fortunate you are to see the things you see!"

---

[5] Robert Schuler, *Tough Minded Faith for Tender Hearted People* (Nashville, TN: Thomas Nelson Publications, 1979), 98.

BOXING

"Hey, Ma, your bad boy done it!
I told you somebody up there likes me."

Rocky Graziano, middleweight champion,
after defeating Tony Zale for the title.

The Parable of the Bee and the Bomber

There was a heavyweight boxing champion who told the world that he "floats like a butterfly and stings like a bee." He also said, "I'm the greatest." There was another heavy-weight boxing champion called the Bronx Bomber, who told the radio audience after every fight, "Another lucky night."

In the parable of the Pharisee and the tax collector,[1] the Pharisee was "the greatest." He did everything he said he did. He was the moral athlete of his day. On the other hand, the tax collector could only say, "God, be merciful to me, a sinner."

The parable is about pride and humility and it is easy to make the assumption that Mohammed Ali is an example of pride, and Joe Louis of humility. However, Mohammed Ali was the greatest, and Joe Louis' luck referred to the fact that anyone can lose. He won by skill and power and not by luck.

The parable is about looking up to higher standards. When we look up, we see our failures. When we look down, the only thing we see is pride. It all depends on what we compare ourselves with. And when we set our lives beside the life of Jesus and beside the Holiness of God, all that is left to say is, "God, be merciful to me, a sinner."[2] Whether we are a bee or a Bomber.

Philippians 2:5-11 - The attitude you should have is the one that Christ Jesus had: etc.

---

[1] Luke 18:9-14.

[2] William Barclay, *The Daily Study Bible Series – The Gospel of Luke* (Philadelphia, PA: The Westminster Press, 1975), 225.

The Parable of the Big Cat

It was a typical Sunday morning; he was re-reading his sermon as he ate breakfast. Then he took a glance at the headlines of the morning newspaper and it said "Big Cat Shot". His reaction was disbelief, then dismay, and then despair, for this was one of his sports heroes. He had to throw away his prepared sermon and respond to the moment.

I was the preacher and the Big Cat was Cleveland Williams. My heavyweight champion was barely hanging onto life. My dreams for him were shattered, but my love continued. I could only think of Hosea's continued love for his unfaithful wife.

The people we love the most need our love the most when they shatter our dreams, destroy our hopes, misuse their freedom, commit a foolish act, or are responsible for a major or minor act of unlovableness.

This parable is the story of the Bible. It is the continuing ways that the people of God have let Him down, and God's love of the unlovable is the continuing message of the Old and New Testaments. It is also God's challenge to you, me and the people of God.

I John 4:10 - This is what love is: It is not that we have loved God, but that he has loved us and sent his Son to be the means by which our sins are forgiven.

The Parable of the Big Fight

The Big Cat lay near death for several weeks, but after months of recuperation, he got his title shot in the Astrodome and I had my ringside seat. The night had finally arrived. The results were obvious when his opponent really could float like a butterfly and sting like a bee. Cleveland Williams was knocked out in the third round. It was over in a hurry because the Cat's great left hook couldn't be allowed a chance. There was no chance and the gunshot proved to make no difference at all.

Normally I would have walked out of the fight tearful and depressed. However, I recognized the greatness of Ali and the courage of the Cat. "The criterion of value, as we tend to define it, is strictly the percentage in the won and lost column, and nothing else. The successful preacher is the one with the biggest church."[3] But my definition of success changed that night. It finds expression now in the Biblical reference below and the words from a most successful coach: "Success is peace of mind which is the direct result of self-satisfaction in knowing you did your best to become the best that you are capable of being."[4]

2 Corinthians 4:8-9 – We are often troubled, but not crushed; sometimes in doubt, but never in despair; there are many enemies, but we are never without a friend; and though badly hurt at times, we are not destroyed.

---

[3] John E. Hines, *Focus on the Cross* (Atlanta, GA: Episcopal Radio-TV Foundation, 1967), 4-5.
[4] Lee Green, *Sportswit*, (New York: Fawcett Crest, 1984), 377.

The Parable of a Tragic Death

Theophilus said, "I love to go to a prize fight, but the dark sides are the tragedies caused by brain damage that produce punch drunk fighters. These are walking tragedies. However, when a fighter is killed in the ring, it is very hard to deal with and come up with an answer."

As a people, we have trouble dealing with trauma, but the most difficult situation for a Christian is to help a friend through a tragic death in the family. Most of the time, just being there is all that is necessary. However, if you feel a need to respond, I hope the following is helpful:

"Why did this happen to us?" "What did we do to deserve this?" "God doesn't give us more than we can bear."

God does not kill people. When someone asks why, the honest to God answer is found in the investigator's report if a violent death occurs.

The second point to be made is that in cases of sickness, we die because our bodies are not able to defeat the disease. Diseases are caused by living in a fallen world. Other problems are caused by mistreating our bodies over a long period of time. Others are caused because our original equipment varies. The causes are all found in an actuarial table and not the will of God.

The final point is, "Don't argue." If a person finds comfort in God as the reason, so be it, Amen. However, the God revealed in Jesus Christ is the Answer and not the Problem.

Luke 12:12 - For the Holy Spirit will teach you at that time what to say.

32

The Parable of the Size of the Dog

The spruiker was braying "Come on, chaps, who'll take a glove? Who wants to have a go? Take a glove, win a fiver." "I will!" Frank shouted, "I will, I will." He shook off Father Ralph's restraining hand as those around them in the throng, seeing Frank's diminutive size, began to laugh and good-naturedly push him to the front. "Don't laugh, gents. He's not very big, but he is the first to volunteer! It isn't the size of the dog in the fight, you know, it's the size of the fight in the dog."[5]

"Most people lose the battle of life by never conquering the fear of failure enough to attempt to climb the biggest challenges God puts before them. They never even step into the ring! They were knocked out before the first round."[6]

We take our first step in life, we fail. With parental encouragement we get up, trying again. Trying again and again is true in all games. In sports, half the teams lose.

As a Christian, you fail more than you succeed. Your witness is ineffective. Your counseling is a failure. Your advice is not heard. "Love never gives up, and its faith, hope and patience never fail."[7]

I Corinthians 9:27 - I harden my body with blows and bring it under complete control, to keep myself from being disqualified after having called others to the contest.

---

[5] Colleen McCullough, *The Thorn Birds* (New York: Harper and Row, 1977), 93-94.
[6] Robert Schuler, *Tough-Minded Faith for Tender Hearted People* (Nashville, TN: Thomas Nelson Publications, 1979).
[7] I Corinthians 13:7.

The Parable of the Left Jab

A priest took a friend to his first boxing match. The friend wanted to know the meaning of everything. The color on the corners, the referee's instructions, the mouthpiece. Before one bout a fighter crossed himself and the friend promptly said, "What does that mean?" The priest replied, "It doesn't mean anything if he doesn't have a left jab."[8]

Many people believe that various shows of piety in some way or other protect them from "...the changes and chances of this mortal life."[9] Religious acts may put a person in the right attitude to succeed, but they are not the main reason for success in any endeavor.

Winning begins with God-given talent. Winning then requires using that talent. Winning requires self-discipline, training, and good coaching. Winning means establishing goals. Winning means learning to do our job well by recognizing the limitations that we have and compensating for them.

The same is true of the Christian life. We can't preach what we haven't practiced, and only by developing our talents can we practice what we preach.

I Corinthians 9:26b - . . . that is why I am like a boxer who does not waste his punches.

---

[8] Adapted from a story I heard on the radio.
[9] *The Book of Common Prayer* (New York: The Church Hymnal Corporation, 1979), 832.

The Parable of One-Eyed Connelly

"In the early days of boxing One-Eyed Connelly was a promoter and heavy better as he traveled from big fight to big fight. He had a habit of losing his glass eye in a store and offering a $500 reward for its return. He would leave and a confederate would show up, find the eye, and then be offered $100 for it by someone expecting to make a nice profit. The entrepreneur would then hurry to Connelly and proffer the eye only to be told it was the wrong one. Connelly would split the hundred with his pal. They kept a stock of glass eyes for just such an occasion."[10]

The man who was deceived in the con game will later have the typical response, "Why didn't I see this coming?" In other situations a common response would be, "It is so obvious now that I look back at it," or "I should have known better." It has often been said that our hindsight is 20/20.

It is this very hindsight that causes us to blame ourselves for anything that goes wrong. The result is either real or false guilt. Strangely, real guilt is easier to deal with. Real guilt is when the result is obviously my fault. False guilt latches onto the way it could have been avoided.

Quite often the person that we con the most is ourself.

Proverbs 19:3 - Some people ruin themselves by their own stupid actions and then blame the Lord.

---

[10] Lee N. Miletich, *Dan Stuart's Fistic Carnival* (College Station, TX: Texas A & M University Press, 1994), from Corbett, *Roar of the Crowd*, 226-227.

FOOTBALL

*"Outlined against a blue-gray October sky
the four horsemen rode again.
In dramatic lore they are known as
famine, pestilence, destruction and death –
their real names are
Stuhldreher, Miller, Crowley and Layden."*

❈

Grantland Rice, writer, describing the
Notre Dame backfield in 1924

The Parable of the Blocked Punt

A certain young English boy moved to the United States. He said, "Exile is an ugly business at any age. (Football) became a shortcut, or substitute, for mastering the local culture. I still didn't know how to talk to these people but while I was playing I didn't have to. The soundless pat on the back, the nice going, Sheed - you could be any manner of clod, or even an English boy, and it didn't matter. I remember blocking a punt with my stomach and writhing in agony and feeling it was worth it for the brief respect I commanded."[1]

Being a member of a team is a great example of what St. Paul meant by members of the Church. "He meant what we should call organs, things essentially different from, and complementary to, one another: things differing not only in structure and function but also in dignity."[2]

We are all different, we have different positions, different roles. The quarterback can't say to the tight end, I have no need of you. The star can't say to the special team player, you're not important. Each is different, each contributes, each takes a kick in the stomach and each has his moments, "Nice going, Sheed."

I Corinthians 12:12-26 – One body with many parts.

---

[1] Wilfred Sheed, *The Morning After* (New York, Farrar, Straus, and Giroux, 1971), 97.
[2] C. S. Lewis, *The Weight of Glory* (New York: The MacMillan Company, 1949), 33.

The Parable of First Downs

A certain uncle said to his nephew, "Remember what I've always said to you. A lot of first downs will take you to the land of six." "That's right," said the nephew. "First downs, nephew," the uncle said. "O.K.," he said.[3]

In the day-to-day work of being a Christian, it is necessary to grind it out. You learn by trying this and then trying that. Quite often you are thrown for a loss. At other times, you get hurt and you have to sit on the sidelines for a time. Many seek the razzle-dazzle experience (the "Hail Mary" pass). This is spectacular when it occurs, but it occurs on limited occasions. The most common Christian pilgrimage is made on three yards and a cloud of dust.

Lou Holtz said, "A successful life is built on a series of successful days. A successful game is built on a series of successful, consistent plays."[4]

A Christian life is built on the fundamentals, the game plan. It consists not in the extraordinary but the ordinary. It begins with church attendance, a sacramental life, daily prayer, stewardship of time and money. You may not be able to tell everyone about your big day, but you will cross the goal.

Hebrews 12:1b - . . . and let us run with determination the race that lies before us.

---

[3] Dan Jenkins, *Semi-Tough* (New York: Athenaeum, 1972), 195.
[4] Lou Holtz, *Corpus Christi Caller Times*, Aug. 6, 1980.

The Parable of the Red Zone

Theophilus used parables to teach them many things. He stated that football teams find it easy to make first downs when the defense is spread all over the field. However, when they get inside the opponent's twenty yard line (the Red Zone) it becomes difficult to score because the defenses are more stacked against them.

People discover as they progress down the field of Christian understanding and ethics, the questions become more difficult. When the rules are basically "Thou shalt Not", the demands are simple and being a "good" Christian is relatively easy. They become more difficult when they move from "Thou shalt not" to "Thou shalt". Most haven't committed the overt act of murder, but how many haven't gotten angry?[5]

Take this test on personal almsgiving. Give a very large sum of money to a worthy cause and not tell anyone what you did. Then see how long it takes you to think "My, what a wonderful person I am . . . I gave all that money and I didn't even tell anyone."

The broad laws narrow down to the spirit of the law. They move from ethics of law to ethics of grace, which places you on difficult ground. It's hard to score points, because you are in the Red Zone.

Mark 10:26-27 – "Who then can be saved?" Jesus looked straight at them and answered, "This is impossible for man, but not for God; everything is possible for God."

---

[5] Matthew 5:22-23.

The Parable of the Unprepared

A certain football coach told this parable: "Luck is what happens when preparation meets opportunity."[6]

Among the parables of Jesus, one of the favorites of the early church was the Parable of the Ten Virgins because they waited expectantly for the Bridegroom (The Second Coming). For me it is a parable on being prepared for our opportunities. The wise are ready.

About forty years ago I heard an old story about a preacher. He was having trouble preparing sermons. A minister friend told him that all he had to do was pray to God to speak to him - enter the pulpit and a great sermon would flow from his lips. The next Sunday, he tried it and his friend, anxious to know what happened, called the preacher and said, "Did God speak to you?" "Oh, yes, He spoke!" said the preacher. "Well, what did he say?" asked the friend. The preacher paused and replied, "God said to me, 'Jack, you're lazy!'"

When opportunity comes, there are always people who say, "Give us some of your oil," this a common request in different words, and it would seem to be the Christian thing to do, but you can't give someone else your preparation.

Matthew 25: 1-13 - The Parable of the Ten Virgins

---

[6] Denne H. Freeman, *Hook 'Em Horns* (Huntsville, AL: Strode Publishers, 1974), 185. Quote of Darrell Royal.

The Parable of the Talents

A certain coach called his staff together and told them this parable. "Each of you will hit the highways and byways of this state looking for the high school athletes who will make our program. You have seen many of their talents on film, but I remind you we need to get as many five-talent players as possible. Also keep your eyes open for those who can help us on special teams and the kicking game."

A great team requires five-talent players. These are the players who have: (1) size, (2) speed, (3) mobility, (4) character and (5) durability. Some five-talent players bury their talents and become a deficit to the team. The superstar works to develop his talents. In many cases, he works harder than anyone on the team; he does not allow his many talents to carry him for he must carry others.

"God never demands from a man abilities which he has not got; but He does demand that we should use the full ability which we possess. Men are not equal in talent; but men can be equal in effort."[7]

If you go to a professional football practice, you will usually see two people working alone. They may even be on a different practice field. Usually these two players have only one talent. However, their efforts decide as many football games as the five-talent running back. They are the punter and the field goal/conversion kickers.

Matthew 25:14-30 - The Parable of the Talents

---

[7] William Barkley, *The Daily Study Bible Series – The Gospel of Matthew*, Vol. 2 (Philadelphia: The Westminster Press, 1975), 323.

The Parable of Spontaneity

Theophilus said, "Look at a football team, it practices the same plays over and over again. Each player learns his assignment, where to go, who to block, or how to take someone out of the play. The ball carrier learns every step he is supposed to take to reach the hole in the line of scrimmage. He then is told nothing after reaching the hole. He's either going to stick himself on the linebacker, or he's going to make smoke and reach the goal line. But it's his baby, nobody tells him what to do then."[8]

Spontaneity comes only after a person has mastered the basics. Saint Augustine said, "Love God and do what you will." This takes a lot of practice in the ways of loving God.

The great backs can cut across the grain to make the goal line. Jesus cut across the rules of husking corn on the Sabbath.[9]

So first come the plays, then comes the practice, then comes calling the right play in the right situation, then comes the spontaneity.

John 8:31b-32 – "If you obey my teaching, you are really my disciples; you will know the truth, and the truth will set you free."

---

[8] Neil Amour, *The Fifth Down* (New York: Ward, McCann and Geoghegan, Inc., 1971), 260.
[9] Mark 2:23-28.

44

The Parable of Both

A certain National Football League owner[10] asked one of his players[11], "Do you want to play football or baseball?" The player responded, "Both." "Defense or Offense?" "Both." The owner said, "Do you want stuffed crust or plain?" The player again said, "Both." The owner's final question was, "Do you want $15 million or $20 million?" The player concluded with "Both."[12]

In the Parable of the Rich Fool[13] the younger brother wanted "both." He wanted his part of the inheritance, but he also wanted half of his older brother's inheritance which was twice as much by Jewish law. Jesus' answer was to warn the younger brother against greed, and in the process to also warn us. In a poor nation, the people want something to eat. In a rich nation, the people want more than they need. This greed, covetousness, avarice are the triple-threats that endanger professional athletes. If a player has to be suspended and fined, who cares? "I've got more than enough." The demise of professional sports will be caused by the greed that prices everyone else out of being a part. Free agents move, teams move, and loyalty will move to other interests.

I Timothy 6:9 - But those who want to get rich fall into temptation and are caught in the trap of many foolish and harmful desires, which pull them down to ruin and destruction.

---

[10] Jimmy Jones, Owner of the Dallas Cowboys.
[11] Deon Sanders, Defensive Back/Wide Receiver, Dallas Cowboys.
[12] A telephone advertisement for Pizza Hut.
[13] Luke 12:13-24.

The Parable of the Member

There was once a minister who called on a member of the church. After visiting, the minister said, "I need to go home to watch the Cowboys." The member said, "I love the Cowboys." The minister replied, "I can't stand the Cowboys." The member responded, "I'm so glad to hear that." The minister asked, "Why?" The member said, "Now I have a good reason not to come to Church."

As we go through life, most institutions, groups, or organizations are called "ours". It is our team, our town, our school, our bank, our club. There are exceptions but it seems to me that the most common is "my" church.

Everything in "my" church has to be perfect except me. Every decision has to agree with my opinion. If "my" minister does anything or says anything that I disagree with, he or she becomes "their" minister.

This is like the toe saying to the hand, "If you scratch me, I'm leaving." If you see yourself as an organ in the Body of Christ, you can't leave. "That structural position in the Church which the humblest Christian occupies is eternal and even cosmic. The Church will outlive the universe; in it the individual person will outlive the universe. Everything that is joined to the immortal Head will share His immortality."[14]

I Corinthians 12:27 - All of you are Christ's body, and each one is part of it.

---

[14] C. S. Lewis, *The Weight of Glory* (New York: The MacMillan Co., 1949), 39.

The Parable of the Unjust School Board

Theophilus said to his students, "There was a federal judge who said a certain town had to desegregate its dual school system. The town had three high schools and one was composed of ninety-nine percent minority students. The school board decided the quickest, surest way to desegregate was to close the minority school. Once the plan was announced, a hotly debated aspect was -- which of the two remaining high schools would get the greater number of black football players.[15] They decided to send them to the school with the traditionally best football team. It was gerrymandering over football." And Theophilus commended the school board for its prudence.

Needless to say, Theophilus is not recommending that you act like the school board. The people in parables are just people -- some good -- some bad. But like Jesus, Theophilus takes a quality, a truth, and turns it into a statement about the God - man relationship. Theophilus says, "I wish Christians were as ingenuous for Christian purposes as the school board was for their own purpose."

Luke 16:1-13 - This parable is a rewrite of the Parable of the Dishonest Steward who stores up favors with his clients by cheating the boss - and Jesus praises the dishonest steward for his foresight and shrewdness.

---

[15] H. G. Bissinger, *Friday Night Lights* (Reading, MA: Addison-Wisley Publishing Co., Inc. 1990), 105.

The Parable of the Gipper

Lying on his deathbed in a hospital, a certain football player[16] said to his coach, "Sometimes, Rock, when the team's up against it, when things are going wrong and the breaks are beating the boys, tell them to go in there with all they've got and win just one for the Gipper. I don't know where I'll be then, Rock, but I'll know about it."[17]

Chet Grant, a teammate of Gipp's, says that Rock actually pulled the "win one for the Gipper" stunt for the first time at the 1921 Indiana game, the year after George Gipp died. Lore links it to the 1928 Army game.

It is hard to say what turns a team around. It could be an inspirational speech. It could be a mental mistake by the opponent. It could be a bad call by the referees.

It is hard to say what turns a person around, when he is up against it. It has been my experience that these moments occur when the right person is in the right place at the right time and says the right thing. This is why it is important for Christians to be responsive to need. It could be merely a "yes" to the need for help. It could be the right theology in the moment of despair. It could be even a letter to the Church in Corinth.

I Corinthians 5:3 - And even though I am far away from you in body, still I am there with you in spirit.

---

[16] George Gipp.
[17] Jack Newcombe, ed., *The Fireside Book of Football* (New York: Simon and Schuster, 1964), 364.

The Parable of Tradition

Theophilus told this parable to those who wondered why the same teams seemed to have winning programs year after year: A young boy asked his father, "Dad, why does our high school football team win almost every game?" The dad replied, "Because we always have."

In the 1930's our high school football team came to their home games in a rather small moving van. After every game, the team climbed back in the van and sang the school song, which began, "Our Alma Mater, from you we've learned to be, so proud of your traditions, your spirit, loyalty."

The tradition produced one of the top won-lost records in the history of Texas high school football. Thirty-four years after I graduated from high school, my son saw me listening to the radio and I was crying. He said, "Dad, what happened? What's the matter?" I said, "Temple just won the State Championship."

Tom Landry, former coach of the Dallas Cowboys said, "A lot of winning is tradition."[18]

II Thessalonians 2:15 – So then, brethren, stand firm and hold to the traditions which you were taught by us, either by word of mouth or by letters.
King James Version.

---

[18] Red Barber, *The Broadcaster* (New York: The Dial Press, 1970), 225.

The Parable of the Turnover

Theophilus said, "In football an extra point is called a conversion, but I would call a turnover a conversion."

In life we constantly try to turn faith into works, but we just can't be saved by our effort. Our question is, "Who, then, can be saved?" Jesus looked straight at them and answered, "This is impossible for man but not for God; everything is possible for God."[19]

I am asked, "If being good doesn't save you, then why try?" If a person believes that he has to be good in order to be loved, he is all mixed up and usually his relationships are, too. It is love that produces goodness; it is not goodness that produces love.

To view the Christian life as a series of scoring extra points with God is to miss the point. The Christian life is turning over my salvation to God, responding in gratitude for the gift of unconditional love and finally being able to hear Jesus say, "The servant does not deserve thanks for obeying orders, does he?" It is the same with you; when you have done all you have been told to do, say, "We are ordinary servants; we have only done our duty."[20]

Galatians 2:16b – For no one is put right with God by doing what the law requires.

---

[19] Mark 10:27.
[20] Luke 17:10b.

The Parable of Ten Days in August

A certain football coach[21] took his football team to a small town in August. It was very hot and very dry. They went on six buses, but came back in only two. The team dwindled from about ninety players to twenty-nine. Years later, the coach set up a $100,000 scholarship for the descendants of the survivors.[22]

This is about the most grueling training program any football team had to endure, as far as I know. It reflected an attitude captured in the saying, "When the going gets tough, the tough get going." Anyone who played sports over 40 years ago experienced belt lines, laps, and other forms of "discipline" which were not considered cruel and unusual punishment. I use the word discipline because it was not viewed as punishment but understood as a natural consequence of whatever I or we did wrong.

The most difficult part of parenting today is that many don't know the difference between discipline and punishment. Discipline is saying what you mean and meaning what you say. If you don't mean it, don't say it. I hear threats but no action, which is so unfair to the child. Then frustration comes and a child is punished for not doing what they were told, but the offenders were the parents who didn't do what they told.

Ephesians 6:4 – Parents, do not treat your children in such a way as to make them angry. Instead, raise them with Christian discipline and instruction.

---

[21] Coach Paul "Bear" Bryant at Texas A & M.
[22] David Halberstam, *The Best American Sports Writing, 1991* (Boston: Houghton Mifflin Company, 1991) 82.

The Parable of the Line Coach

Theophilus said: "A certain line coach was called into the service for duty in World War II. The coach came home on leave after serving in Europe. He arrived home on a Friday night and quite unexpectedly walked on the field. At first a few saw him and a buzz began, then with the roar of the crowd the team rallied and transformed an apparent defeat into victory."

This event happened years ago and remains vividly in my mind. It has always been for me an example of how an outside force can cause others to rise to the occasion. It is the best example of leaven that I ever saw.

"Leaven is any substance that causes the dough to rise in baking." (The kind most familiar to us is yeast.) Leaven is a very apt illustration of the way in which an influence, good or bad, can spread.[23] Rabbis often associated fermentation with corruption, while the early Christian used it to describe the power of the Holy Spirit.

Today, Christians by life and witness are called to be leaven. The occasions are numerous when a Christian is called to rise to the opportunity. Those occasions are best capsuled in St. Francis' famous prayer:

"Where there is hatred, let me sow love;
Where there is doubt, pardon,
Where there is despair, hope,
Where there is darkness, light . . ."

I Corinthians 5:6b – A little bit of yeast makes the whole batch of dough rise.

---

[23] F. B. Magnutt, *The Prayer Manual* (Oxford, England: A. R. Mowbry, 1957), 9.

The Parable of a Record of 7-3

A certain football coach[24] said, "I like losing three games in a season better than just losing one. The fans talk about the games you won after a 7-3 season. When you go 9-1, they talk about the one you lost."[25]

When a person is attractive, smart, articulate, athletic, president of the class, popular and has musical talents, then it is quite natural to concentrate our attention on some fault. They run like this, "She's not as pretty as she thinks she is!" or "He's not really that smart," or "She can make a good speech, but have you ever tried to have a conversation with her?" or "He's good, but he can't shoot free throws any better than I can."

When a person is rather unattractive, we say, "She's not too pretty, but she sure has a good personality." "He doesn't make good grades, but he has a lot of good old common sense."

When we look at those with a record worse than ours this makes us feel better. However, it also keeps us from accomplishing as much as we should. "The greatest enemy of the best is the good." Most people had rather be 7-3 than 9-1 because it requires less of us. And we would rather look at our wins than our losses.

I Corinthians 15:41b - . . . and even among stars there are different kinds of beauty.

---

[24] Coach Doug Dickey, Florida Coach.
[25] Lee Green, *Sportswit*, (New York: Harper and Row, 1984), 108.

The Parable of Putting On

A man said, "Look over there! That must be a team that is traveling to a game." His wife said, "How can you tell?" The husband replied, "Because they all have on coats and ties." A person who overheard the conversation said, "They're just putting-on."

In the parable of the wedding garment, the king said to a man brought in off the street, "Friend, how did you get in here without wedding clothes?"[26] Before you start feeling too sorry for this man, look around and you see everyone else brought in off the street has on wedding clothes. This man must have ignored the free tuxedo rental right there in the Palace.

It is sometimes possible to tell who is going to win a game just by the way a team dresses. If they look sharp they play sharp. When they look sloppy they play sloppy.

There is another side of the fact that we act like we dress. Darrell Royal said (on fancy striped uniforms), "Hell, no, I'm not going to candy things up. These are work clothes."[27]

In the parable of the Prodigal Son, the first thing that the father says is, "Bring quickly, the best robe, and put it on him."[28] The lost son still has the dirt from the pigpen on him, but he has the robe of sonship on him and he feels good.

Ephesians 4:23-24a - Your hearts and minds must be made completely new, and you must put on the new self.

---

[26] Matthew 22:12.
[27] Denne Freeman, *Hook 'Em Horns* (Huntsville, AL: Strode Publishers, 1974), 182.
[28] Luke 15:22.

The Parable of the Diagram

Theophilus said, "When any football coach wants to show his team a play, he draws a diagram on a blackboard. In this way each player can see what everyone is expected to do."[29]

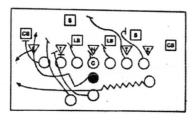

The diagram shows where twenty-two men are likely to be and what the offensive players are supposed to do. The play is called a quarterback option because he has the choice of which back will carry the ball. This picture is acted out on the playing field day after day, and then used in a game.

This is a parable. The play is drawn on a blackboard or put into a playbook because you need to be able to see it in order to get the picture. "By reducing the scale of events, it can introduce much larger events."[30]

When we grasp the concept that you can only understand a football play in a very small diagram, when we understand that you can represent very big ideas in a very small space, then perhaps we'll understand why the first time we see God is in a manger.

John 1:14a - The Word became a human being and, full of grace and truth, lived among us.

---

[29] Bob Reade, *Coaching Football Successfully* (Champaign, IL: Human Kinetics Publishers, 1974), 98.
[30] G. K. Chesterton, *Tremendous Tifles* (New York: Dodd, Mead and Company, 1910), 183.

The Parable of Statistics

A certain team had twenty first downs and their opponent had twelve. They also gained 285 net yards to their opponent's 200. The team's fans said, "We beat them every way but on the scoreboard." The winner's fans replied, "They keep statistics for the losers."

It is conceivable that a team could win a game and not make a first down or gain a net yard. The team could score many points with defense and special teams.

However, statistics make the losers feel that we were better than they were.

Habakkuk didn't question the Lord punishing Judah for her sins, but why in the world would they be conquered by the Chaldeans who were much worse?

We wonder why she of all people got the promotion over me! We wonder how he could have possibly beaten me in the election. These are all logical questions, but when "if onlys" and "what might have beens" are carried and dwelt upon they keep us from doing better in the future.

So whatever happens in your life, when you come up short as a spouse, a parent, a Christian, as a human being, the best antidote to keep your past in perspective is "They keep statistics for losers."

I Corinthians 15:10b - I have worked harder than any of the other apostles, although it was not really my own doing, but God's grace working with me.

The Parable of Half Lose

A certain college coach said, "You go out and recruit your ass off, set 'em up in a dorm where you can get at 'em whenever you want, keep 'em eligible, feed 'em, run 'em in the off-season program, get 'em summer jobs that will keep them in shape, stay up nights figuring plays, go blind over films, woo boosters, argue with professors, scout by computers, and God knows what else. And what happens, half the teams go out and lose every week."[31]

While the chant, "We're Number One" rings out of many stadiums on a fall afternoon, the fact remains there is only one Number One (except when the voters disagree).

A common accolade is, "They know how to win." It is also important to "know how to lose."

Many parents try to protect their children from the agony of defeat by blaming someone else. However, accepting defeat is important to understanding life.

Losing seasons build character. I've seen very little character in players who never faced adversity. A lot of young people really never had to struggle for anything in their lives. When it finally happens the character isn't there to get them through. What do they turn to? Alcohol, drugs, you name it.[32]

Romans 12:15 - Be happy with those who are happy, and weep with those who weep.

---

[31] Neil Amour, *The Fifth Down – Democracy and the Football Revolution* (New York: Ward, McCann and Geoghegan, Inc., 1971), 259.

[32] Jack Clary, *The Game Makers, A National Football League Book* (Chicago: Follett Publishing Company, 1976), 1.

The Parable of the 12th Man

Theophilus told the parable of a certain football player[33] who broke his leg in the final game of the 1921 season. Another player[34] had quit the team to play basketball, but was used as a football spotter for the bowl game. The coach[35] sent word to the basketball player/spotter at the half to suit up, as he might be needed. He swapped clothes with an injured player; thus began the tradition of the 12th man.[36]

This parable is about tradition and readiness to serve. Most traditions come out of an event. Traditions are born, not made. The tradition of the 12th man came out of a special need, and for many years the corps of cadets have stood at Aggie football games.

For Christians, the first 12th man was Matthias, chosen to replace Judas as an apostle. He is but the first in a long tradition of those who are willing to come out of the crowd and say they have met the Risen Lord.

Many will "stand up, stand up, for Jesus," while singing in the stands (pews); very few of us are willing to "put on the divine armor-truth for a belt, righteousness for breastplate, readiness to affirm the gospel for shoes, faith for shield, and the inspired word of God for sword."[37]

Isiah 6:8 – I heard the Lord say, "Whom shall I send? Who will be my messenger?" I answered, "I will go! Send me!"

---

[33] Harry T. Pinson.
[34] E. King Gill.
[35] Dana X. Bible.
[36] Dan Cook, *San Antonio Express News*, (Saturday) 15 September 1990.
[37] Ephesians 6:14-16.

The Parable of Ties

A certain coach said, "A tie is like kissing your sister," and his female assistant said, "No, a tie is like kissing your brother." The coach replied, "Either way, it is not a satisfactory result."

A faith assumption of football is that there shouldn't be a tie. The strange result of this is that regardless of the many plans on how to break a tie they are all called "sudden death."

The attitude permeates every area of American life. In foreign policy the Monday morning quarterbacks want victory, one way or another, while the President bears responsibility for the consequences.

Many of our human relationships, such as marriage and divorce, parent and child, end in sudden death because we want the problem solved or we want out. We have great difficulty living with unresolved conflicts. There are many problems in a marriage which can't be solved.

It is a serious problem when our philosophy of sports replaces our Christian understanding of life; love doesn't keep score.

Matthew 13:24-30, 36-43 - The Parable of the Wheat and the Tares.

The Parable of Luck

A certain football player said, "Your good luck is usually the other team's bad luck. Injuries are good luck and bad luck . . . Luck can be someone clipping your free safety and the official not seeing the play. Luck can be recovering a fumble that an official said was a dead ball or catching a pass that should have been called incomplete. Because of the high level of competition it takes luck to win."[38]

We make our own luck. However, luck is a constant factor in our lives. Some call it fate, predestination, some call it being born with a silver spoon in your mouth. "There are coaches who spend eighteen hours a day coaching the perfect game. And they lose because the ball is oval and they can't control the bounce."[39]

We need to remember that God did not make the football oval. Bringing ourselves to acknowledge that there are some things God does not control, many good things become possible. We will be able to turn to God for things He can do to help us, instead of holding on to unrealistic expectations of Him which will never come about.[40]

Bad luck or good luck I can cause, but not always. It is often just the way the ball bounces.

The Book of Job.

---

[38] John David Tatum and Bill Kushner, *They Call Me Assassin*, (New York: Everest House Publishers, 1979), 141.
[39] Bud Grant, <u>Viking Coach</u>, *Corpus Christi Caller Times*, 28 July 1980.
[40] Harold S. Kushner, *When Bad Things Happen to Good People* (New York: Schocken Books, 1981), 45.

The Parable of the Dance

Theophilus said, "A certain coach was asked what his plan was for the upcoming game. He said, 'We're gonna dance with the ones who brung us.'"[41]

It would be difficult for most Christians to define Christianity. It is many things to many people. It finds expression in many forms, ranging from the social gospel to spirituality. For some it is the Word; for others it is the Sacraments. As one goes from church to church and denomination to denomination, we find so many varieties that most of us could and would say, "I couldn't belong to that church!"

As we try over and over to find more relevant expressions of Christianity, we need to be reminded that we should dance with the ones who brung us.

"What is Christianity? If one turns to the great classical tradition one finds absolute unanimity about what Christianity is: it is the story of the Bible. This story has been put in condensed form and symbolic language in the great creeds and classical Catholic or classical Protestant statements of faith."[42]

This is what brung us!

Ecclesiastes 1:9 - What has happened before will happen again. What has been done before will be done again. There is nothing new in the whole world.

---

[41] Denne H. Freeman, *Hook 'Em Horns* (Huntsville, AL: Strode Publishing House, 1964), 17. Quote from Darrell Royal.
[42] A. T. Mollegan, *The Faith of Christians* (Washington, D.C.: Henderson Service, 1953), 5.

GOLF

*"Don't hurry, don't worry.
You're only here on a short visit, so don't forget to
stop and smell the flowers."*

❈

Walter Hagen, professional golfer,
on how to live

The Parable of the Lost Golf Ball

A certain golfer had a one-stroke lead as she prepared to hit her tee shot on the 18th tee box. She hit a horrendous hook that headed for a dense area of trees and foliage. It looked out of bounds, so she hit a provisional drive that split the fairway. As she and her caddie trudged down the fairway, they reached the point where they last saw the first drive. They searched and searched for the lost drive, but had to give up and return to the fairway. With the two-stroke penalty for going out of bounds, the tournament would likely be lost. Then on the way back, the caddie spotted the lost ball. It had hit a tree and bounced back in bounds.

The parable is, of course, the parable of the lost coin. So the golfer says, "Rejoice with me for I have found the drive that I thought was lost." There is more joy in heaven over the one golf ball that was lost and found than over the seventeen drives that landed on the greens or fairways.

Christian education has three steps, and these steps can be taken in any order, but all three are necessary. It can begin with the parable of the lost coin. The second step can be to put these words in my own words - the parable of the lost golf ball. The third step can be to realize that I am the golf ball. I have found that in many parables I identify with the wrong person or thing.

See: Luke 15:8-10 - The Parable of the Lost Coin.

The Parable of the Putter

Behold, the golfer on the green. He looks at his putt from every side. He tries to read the green - every angle, every slope, every undulation. He then gets behind his golf ball and looks at the cup - he determines the speed and finally he can get a picture of the rolling ball and imagine the putt being sunk. If he thinks he'll miss, he will.

Imagination is God's gift to us so that we might witness the unseen. This is the positive truth in the value of positive thinking. If there is a plank eighteen inches wide lying on the ground, most any of us can walk it. If we raise that same plank in the air, very few can walk it. The difference is that on the ground we picture ourselves succeeding; in the air, we picture ourselves failing.

If I see the Lord as my Shepherd, He will be. If I hope that someday He will be, He won't.

If you wait until you are a Christian to start acting like one, then you'll never become one. However, if you start acting like one, then you'll become one before you know it.

Romans 6:11 - In the same way you are to think of yourself as dead, so far as sin is concerned, but living in fellowship with God through Christ Jesus.

The Parable of the 8-Iron

A certain golfer[1] was playing his third shot on the sixteenth at Firestone Country Club and asked his caddie what club to use.

Caddie: "Well, yesterday I caddied for another golfer[2] and he hit an 8-iron."

The golfer proceeded to hit an 8-iron, only to see his ball disappear into the lake in front of the green.

Golfer: "Do you mean to tell me Hebert hit an 8-iron here?"

Caddie: "Yes, sir, he did."

Golfer: "Where'd he hit it?"

Caddie: "Oh, he hit it into the lake, too."[3]

In the making of any choice, the Christian is required to consider two things. First, getting the issues straight, next getting the facts straight; then he can draw a swift conclusion.[4]

The issue is how to get his ball on the green. The fact that is missing is did the other golfer get on the green.

In any decision you make, the first question is where you want your decisions to end up; then decide the best way to get there.

Matthew 27:17 - So when the crowd gathered, Pilate asked them, "Which one do you want me to set free for you? Jesus Barabbas or Jesus called the Messiah?"

---

[1] Sam Snead.

[2] Jay Hebert

[3] Lee Green, *Sportswit* (New York: Fawcett Crest, 1984), 11-12.

[4] James A. Pike, *The Next Day* (Doubleday and Company, Inc., 1957), 49.

The Parable of the Mulligan

A golfer got ready to hit a drive off the first tee. He took a few practice swings and addressed the ball. He hit a wicked slice out of bounds. His opponent said, "You can have a Mulligan." He hit his second drive 200 yards down the middle of the fairway.

"Thomas Mulligan, the Fourth Earl of Murphy, was born in 1793, but his gift, which bears his name, has been a great blessing to the average golfer."[5] His gift was the practice of giving a Mulligan on the first tee box.

Anyone who tries to lead a Christian life experiences mulligans, as God allows us the opportunity to swing again. As in golf, we get a mulligan whenever we attempt a round of anything. Mulligans in God's language are called forgiveness. An opportunity to start over.

So if you get out of bounds with a person, preferably a golfer, and want to get back on a fairway, you might try asking for a mulligan.

How many mulligans do you get? At least 70 x 7 is par for the course.

Hebrews 8:7 - If there had been nothing wrong with the first covenant, there would have been no need for a second one.

---

[5] Information from a letter advertising Mulligan – Golf Sportswear, March 26, 1996.

The Parable of the Handicap

Theophilus told this parable, "A certain son went out to play golf with his father. The son was an excellent golfer and had played on his college team; the father took up the game when he retired. On that day, the father won the match."

Golf is one of the few athletic games, if not the only game, where anyone can win. The amateur can beat the professional, the ninety-year-old can beat the twenty-year-old, the women can beat the men.

The reason is called a handicap - it equalizes the chances of winning. Based on my previous scores and the ranking of difficulty of the course, I am given a stroke for the number of shots that I am over par. Each hole is valued on degree of difficulty and strokes are also awarded in this way.

In life, a handicap makes success more difficult, and it is impossible to make a level playing field. Following the example of Christ whose ministry was basically healing and teaching, a Christian is called to help the handicapped finish the course with less difficulty.

John 5:7b – "Sir, I don't have anyone here to put me in the pool when the water is stirred up; while I am trying to get in, somebody else gets there first."

The Parable of the Cleanest Game

A certain golfer[6] said, "We have the cleanest professional sport of all. In baseball, if a guy traps a ball, he doesn't call it on himself, he tries to fool the umpire. We police ourselves. I've seen people call two-stroke penalties on themselves when it meant a $150,000 tournament."[7]

There is the obvious contrast between the player who knows he fumbled, fouled the opponent, or touched the net, and the golfer who moves a twig, the ball moves, and he calls a one-shot penalty. A judgment call by officials and a rules violation are very different. Calling a rules violation against yourself is an admirable features of golf, but it is unfair to compare it to judgment calls.

In our Christian life we are told, "Children, it is your Christian duty to obey your parents, for this is the right thing to do."[8] This is a good rule if children have good parents. Parental authority becomes a judgment call when their parental judgment is questionable.

In golf the game is the cleanest, except in the very few exceptions like whether or not you get a free drop (a judgment call). In your ethical decisions don't confuse the rules and the judgment calls.

II Corinthians 13:7 - We pray to God that you will do no wrong - not in order to show that we are a success, but so that you may do what is right, even though we may seem to be failures.

---

[6] Bruce Crampton.
[7] Andrew J. Maikovich, *Sports Quotations* (Jefferson, NC: McFarland and Company, Inc., 1984), 1352.
[8] Ephesians 6:1.

The Parable of the Bad Lie

A famous golfer[9] was struck by a terminal illness. A friend asked him if he would recover. "No," he said, "probably not." "But," he added, "we'll say no more about it because, as you know, we play the ball where it lies."[10]

In 1544, Thomas Cranmer wrote a litany that has remained unchanged in Anglican and Episcopal Prayer Books to the present day. One of the petitions that seems most outdated is, "From sudden death, good Lord deliver us." For most Americans sudden death is the way to go in contrast to a prolonged illness. However, I don't know anyone who desires an accidental death.

The chance to leave this world with the ability to tie up loose ends, to say good-bye, and to look with expectation to the life to come opens doors that sudden death slams closed.

Our golfer expressed how Christians should face death in the language of golf. "No bitterness, no self-pity, no raging because you are under the lip of the trap or behind a rock, but the mature soul playing the ball where it lies."[11]

II Timothy 4:7b - I have finished my course, I have kept the faith.
King James Version.

---

[9] Bobby Jones.
[10] Richard S. M. Emrich, *The Theology of Golf* (Cincinnati: Forward Movement Publications, 1992), 10.
[11] Ibid.

HUNTING, FISHING, SAILING

*During the course of a Sunday School session,
the teacher called up one of the pupils to
recite the parable he liked best.
He said, "That's easy, ma'am.
I like the one where someone loafs and fishes."*

Edmund Fuller

The Parable of Old Tip

Theophilus told the crowd another parable. A certain hunter was describing his dog. He said, "As much as I like to see football, I'd leave the Army-Navy game just to see one dog sweeping across a field. The grass and weeds knee high, I watch him come to a perfect point that tells me the quail are right there in front of him. He does not come too close or they would fly away. He does not stop too far away or he could never smell them. It's just one of those things you can't explain."

"In the time of Jesus, the dogs were pariahs, roaming the streets, sometimes in packs, hunting amidst the garbage dumps, and snapping and snarling at all whom they met."[1] This is the reason for the scriptural injunction, "Watch out for those who do evil things, they're dogs..."[2]

The beauty, grace, and discipline of a hunting dog are a sight to see. If Jesus had had the opportunity to see a hunting dog, he would have said, "I wish my servants had this much beauty, grace, and truth so that they could point the way to others."

Mark 1:2b - God said, "I will send my messenger ahead of you to open the way for you."

---

[1] William Barclay, *The Letters to the Philippians, Colossians and Thessalonians* (Philadelphia: The Westminster Press, 1975), 53.
[2] Philippians 3:2.

The Parable of the Cat's-Paw

A fisherman went out in his boat several miles from land. He told me that when he saw a cat's-paw up in the west, he immediately hoisted anchor and headed for home. I asked him what a cat's-paw was. He said, "I can't explain it exactly. But any old time one of the water boys looks up there and sees some of those small whirling clouds having a dance among themselves he immediately changes his own thinking and thinks about land and safety."

In the Bible there are many signs and wonders from nature. The sun and moon.[3] The fig tree.[4] There is the stilling of the storm and the apostles asked, "Who then is this that even wind and sea obey him?"[5]

No one in Jesus' day had even heard of the laws of nature. A miracle was a sign of the power of God. The answer to "Who is this?" was "That's the Lord."

The meaning of the parable of the cat's-paw is that God wishes that men could understand the signs of the times as well as they could read the signs in the sky.

Luke 12:54 - Jesus said also to the people, "When you see a cloud coming up in the west, at once you say that it is going to rain - and it does.

---

[3] Mark 13:24.
[4] Mark 13:28.
[5] Mark 4:41.

The Parable of Against the Wind

A son asked his father, "Daddy, how do sail boats move?" The father said, "When the wind is behind them, they are pushed along. This is called running or sailing downwind." The son replied, "But what happens when they sail against the wind?" The father said, "If the wind is coming from the right side/starboard, you turn the boat right until the wind comes from the new side at an angle of 45 degrees and the wind blowing against the curved surface of the sail produces the aerodynamic situation and the sails become an airfoil."[6]

Christianity's main concern focuses on love, but the most difficult task for all Christians is to be a prophet. We don't hear much about prophecy in the New Testament, but it dominates the Old Testament. The last of the Old Testament prophets in the Bible is found in Jesus' cousin, John the Baptist. Jesus said, When you went out to John in the desert what did you expect to see? A blade of grass bending in the wind?"[7]

A reed shaken in the wind is a Christian who goes in the direction the wind is blowing, who tells someone what they want to hear.

A prophet is not a predictor; he calls us to practice what we preach in our public and private lives. A prophet goes against the wind by revealing the consequences of not mixing politics and religion.

See: Jesus' words about John – Luke 7:14-35.

---

[6] Harvey Frommer and Ron Weinmann, *A Sailing Primer* (New York: Athenaeum, 1978), 42.
[7] Luke 7:24b.

The Parable of Crabbing

Theophilus told the parable of a certain grandfather who took his two grandchildren crabbing. When they caught a particular crab, the grandfather said, "He'll be a soft-shelled crab on the next tide; let's put him in a bucket and watch."

Sure enough, the grandchildren were able to watch the crab shed his hard shell, and also watch the soft shell turn harder and harder. They learned that for a crab to continue to grow it has to become soft each time.

There is meaning in the growth of a crab because God puts meaning everywhere. If we are going to grow as persons there are many times that we have to get out of our protective shell and be placed in a vulnerable position.

A soft-shelled crab has to bury itself in the sand or hide. Vulnerability means death; hiding is the only way to grow up to be an old crab.

Unlike the crab you can only grow as a person by understanding your inability to hide from God and exposing your weakness to Him. In the presence of God, our outer shields are stripped away.

Hebrews 4:13 - There is nothing that can be hid from God; everything in all creation is exposed and lies open before his eyes. And it is to him that we must all give an account of ourselves.

Parable of the Steeplechase

Theophilus said, "One day there was a fox hunt. After a long chase the fox got away. The horsemen then had a race to the next town. As they looked around, the most distinctive feature at a distance was the church steeple, and they raced to the steeple. Since that day, any race over barriers is a steeplechase."[8]

Many times as we race through life, we are in search of a small but definite objective. The opportunity gets away from us and we lose the goal.

As we survey the landscape there are many different options that we can choose in the next city. In the race there is one thing to keep in mind. There is no permanent city for us here on earth; we are looking for the city which is to come.[9]

So when you need to change directions it is not a bad idea to look for a steeple. This will remove your eyes from the trivia of the hunt. There can be this difference; you will review your life against the background of eternity and not live as if the hunt is all that matters.

Colossians 3:1a - If ye then be risen with Christ, seek those things which are above. King James Version

---

[8] *Why Do We Say It?* (Edison, NJ: Castle Books, 1985), 231.
[9] Hebrews 13:14.

MOST SPORTS

"A man must love a thing very much if he not only practices it without any hope of fame and money but even practices it without any hope of doing it well."

G.K. Chesterton - English writer

The Parable of the Rules Committee

Two coaches were discussing the new rules that would go into effect the coming season. One of them said, "I don't know why they have to change the rules every year." The other said, "Well, it might be because we spend a lot of time trying to figure a way to get around the rules."

In every game that is played there is a great need for the rules committee. They meet every year and sometimes more frequently to change the rules.

The reason is that owners, athletic directors, coaches, trainers, and players find ways to get around the rules. Something needs to be defined more clearly, or someone needs to be protected; therefore, the game is changed.

Many people believe that the Biblical rules are eternal and have to stay the same. This misses the point of rules; they are given to help us play the game. There are many referees in this world but don't confuse them with God. It is man, not God, who has determined the penalties.

Some think there are only ten rules; however, these had to be added to, so "the Jewish law contained 248 positive commands and 364 negative commands."[1]

See: Leviticus and Deuteronomy for the many laws.
Matthew 5:17b – I have not come to do away with them, but to make their teachings come true.

---

[1] D. B. J. Campbell, *The Synoptic Gospels* (New York: The Seabury Press, 1966), 106.

The Parable of Jimmy the Greek

Theophilus said, "Let me tell you the story of Jimmy the Greek, who is a famous sports prophet. He tells you the odds by studying every facet of the contest: the previous records, the playing conditions at game time, the home field advantage, the injuries, the different motivational factors, and every detail."

Contrary to popular belief, Jimmy the Greek was not a predictor, he was a prophet. Many sportswriters are predictors; they predict the winners. Jimmy the Greek gave the odds on what would happen unless conditions changed. When conditions changed, the odds changed.

In a similar way, the prophets looked first at the righteousness of God and prophesied that a holy God would not tolerate a sinful people. Thus, they had it 10 to 1 that the Babylonians were going to defeat the Israelites.

The most common misuse of the Bible is to take the great prophesies and apocalyptic writings and use them to predict something that is going to happen shortly. This is like finding an old form sheet to forecast what will happen next season.

I John 4:1 - My dear friends, do not believe all who claim to have the Spirit, but test them to find out if the spirit they have comes from God. For many false prophets have gone out everywhere.

The Parable of "Old Mo"

Theophilus said, "A certain team was playing and it appeared that they would be soundly defeated. Then in the twinkling of an eye, and no one could see why, the game turned around and defeat turned into a remarkable victory."

In sports, "Old Mo" is that invisible but clearly seen factor that inspires a turnaround in any game. The name is Momentum. In church, "Old Mo" is that invisible but clearly seen factor that inspires and turns around a congregation. The name is Holy Spirit.

If you seek the meaning of the Holy Spirit in your life, there is no doubt that another name for the Holy Spirit is "Old Mo." A combination of study, preparation, tradition, esprit de corps produces "Old Mo."

"Poor Old Mo" doesn't even get into the creed until the last paragraph. However, everyone knows that if it weren't for the third paragraph we wouldn't have the first two. On deeper reflection that's the proper place for Mo because if you think you've got Him you lose Him.

John 3:8 – The wind blows wherever it wishes; you hear the sound it makes, but you do not know where it comes from or where it is going.

The Parable of Free Agency

A certain professional athlete completed his contract and decided to become a free agent. He visited one team and they offered him twice as much as his former team, another offered him the same money he was making but a chance to play on a championship team. His old team could not match the offers but his teammates pleaded with him to stay with the old team. Which of the three teams do you think the free agent chose?

When we have choices to make between conflicting desires, we are told to let our conscience be our guide; however, a conscience is nothing more than the values of a society. Those who yelled, "Crucify him!" did so with a very good conscience. A conscience can say, "Take the money. Think of how much good you can do." A conscience says, "You have sacrificed enough to help a poor team be respectable, you don't have to live with the idea that you were good but never won a ring." A conscience says, "Don't be selfish for money or prestige, self-sacrifice is the important thing. Do unto others, and if the star were leaving my team, I'd want him to stay."

Which one did the player choose? He followed the voice of conscience that was most convincing.

Joshua 24:15 - If you are not willing to serve him, decide today whom you will serve . . . As for my family and me, we will serve the Lord.

The Parable of Sin

A certain child asked his father, "What is sin?" The father replied, "In the Biblical language it is an old archery term which means missing the mark. In your language it means you must be a straight shooter."

Sin has become a much bigger idea than that. It includes all the elements that cause a person to miss the mark but goes beyond what each of us do. "Groups are more immoral than individuals."[2]

If you were to ask an individual to give an example of sin, it would usually fall in one of two areas - either vices such as smoking, drinking, gambling, cheating or various sexual activities, or they would say breaking the Ten Commandments.

However, if you look at Christianity to list what sin is - it would be pride, hatred, envy, avarice, sloth, lust, and gluttony - the seven capital sins.

Any of these can destroy a team, and the root cause can always be found here. I wish we didn't live in a society that simplistically looks at the Ten Commandments and says, "I do those," and instead looked humbly at the seven sins and asked, "Why do I do those?" I think we will find that sin is a team sport, whether it is called a company, a gang, a party, or just plain - we.

Romans 3:23 - . . . . everyone has sinned and is far away from God's saving presence.

---

[2] Martin Luther King, Jr., "Letters From Birmington City Jail", *The World Treasury of Modern Religious Thought* (Boston: Little, Brown and Company, 1990), 609.

The Parable of the Three Bones

Theophilus told of the coach who said, "We'll settle for players with three kinds of bones - a funny bone, a wishbone, and a backbone. The funny bone is to enjoy a laugh, even at one's own expense. The wishbone is to think big, set one's goals high and to have dreams and ambitions. The backbone is what a boy needs to go to work and make all those dreams come true."[3]

Many Christians set high goals for themselves. St. Paul tells us to keep on working with fear and trembling toward your salvation.[4] The main shortcoming that we find in most Christians is a lack of a sense of humor. There is little laughing reported in the New Testament, but it's not missing. Jesus jokes about the telephone pole in your eye.[5] On a team, in a family, or a group of friends, there is the need for a sense of humor and mutual trust. The mixture is suspiciously like a word the Bible uses a great deal, the word "love."[6]

However, the three main bones of the Christians are faith, love and hope, and the greatest of these is love.[7]

I Thessalonians 1:3 - For we remember before our God and Father how you put your faith into practice, how your love made you work so hard, and how your hope in our Lord Jesus Christ is firm.

---

[3] Hank Number, *Recruiting in Sports*, (New York: Franklin Watts, 1989), 58.
[4] Philippians 2:12b.
[5] Matthew 7:3.
[6] Herbert O'Driscoll, *One Man's Journey* (Toronto, ON: Anglican Book Centre, 1982), 90.
[7] I Corinthians 13:13.

The Parables of the Kingdom

Theophilus told them these parables:
The Kingdom of heaven is like . . .

✙   making a hole in one

✙   winning a major in tennis or golf

✙   hitting a three pointer with one second on the clock

✙   winning an Olympic medal

✙   catching your biggest fish

✙   being picked number one in a professional draft

Jesus told them these parables. The Kingdom is like a mustard seed,[8] leaven,[9] hidden treasure,[10] a pearl of great value,[11] a lost son.[12]

The Kingdom of heaven is unexpected great joy. However, the parables "can never be more than an intimation of a joy that craves for eternity."[13]

Luke 15:7 – There will be more joy in heaven over one sinner who repents than over ninety nice respectable who do not need to repent.

---

[8] Matthew 13:31.
[9] Matthew 13:33.
[10] Matthew 13:44.
[11] Matthew 13:45.
[12] Luke 15:11-32.
[13] Werner and Lotti Pelz, *God Is No More* (London, England: Victor Gollaez, Inc., 1963), 57.

The Parable of the Defense

Theophilus said, "A certain man never went to see a game, but he watched them religiously on television. He said, "When I watch a game most of the emphasis is on scoring points, but when I read about the game the analysis says the defense determined the outcome of the game."

As one looks at the Christian faith through the centuries we learn the Defenders of the Faith are the heroes of the church. These are emperors and kings, popes and pastors, theologians and philosophers, each a part of our common history.

This is rarely understood because for about five hundred years Christianity has dominated our political, social and economic assumptions in the Western World and it is difficult to distinguish between the sacred and profane.[14] The result is that Christianity is ill-defined and most dialogues are conflicts between denominations, each having its own biblical, credal, sacramental, liturgical, and cultural assumptions and also its own social and political agenda.

An historical perspective helps us to understand our differences and how we got that way. As I have observed the Christian life it is more important to defend your goals than to score points against someone else. To attack what others believe is often quite offensive.

Revelations 3:11b - Keep safe what you have, so that no one will rob you of your victory prize.

---

[14] Read: William A. Clebsch's *From Sacred to Profane America* (New York: Harper and Row Publishers, 1968).

The Parable of Believing

A certain man said, "I don't believe in God." A friend replied, "Then what do you believe in?" The man answered, "I don't believe in anything." His friend said, "Who do you believe is the world's greatest athlete?" He answered, "Babe Didrikson." What do you believe is the best spectator sport?" "Soccer!" His retort was, "Man, you're crazy! Everybody knows it's football!"

Belief is a faith assumption. "When faith becomes 'I know' instead of 'I believe', there is no form of vested interest more abominable than that of religion, religious certainty!"[15]

The main problem in believing is that there are too many gods. "Toys, money, fame, and love were the face of God when they were the most important thing to you. Anything that you believe will bring you final peace and fulfillment is belief, is your version of God."[16] All of these are conflicting gods in the life of most people, even those who believe in Jesus Christ as their Lord and Savior.

In these conflicting beliefs "if people stop believing in religion they don't then believe in nothing, they believe in everything."[17]

Hebrews 11:1 - To have faith is to be sure of the things we hope for, to be certain of things we cannot see.

---

[15] Werner Pelz, *Irreligious reflections of the Christian Church* (Naperville, IL: SCM Book Club, 1959), 122.
[16] Deepek Chapa, *The Way of the Wizard* (New York Harmony Books, 1995), 159.
[17] Margaret Pepper, *The Harper's Religious and Inspirational Quotes* (New York: Harper and Row Publishers, 1989), 49, quotes from G. K. Chesterson.

Parable of the Natural

The sportswriter said, "Have you ever seen, known, or heard of any athlete like that?   He won an Olympic medal on the 400 meter relay team. He is a great wide receiver, he can slam dunk a basketball with the best of them, a great center fielder and a 2 handicap at golf. You've got to say he's a natural."

There is no such thing as a natural; skills are developed. "A winner works his tail off to develop them into skills and uses these skills to accomplish his goal"[18]

When I apply this concept to myself, I can't help but think of the many young people who were like me. We were innately smart enough not to have to study but too dumb to recognize this as a weakness instead of a strength.

Many great athletic talents are wasted because the players are so good that they don't have to work. This is why so many college recruits and professional draft choices · turn out to be mistakes.

The really great talents are those who recognize their weaknesses and work until those weaknesses become strengths.

II Corinthians 12:10b - For when I am weak, then I am strong.

---

[18] Steph Donadid, Joan Smith, Susan Mesner, and Rebecca Davison, ed., *The New York Public Library Book of 20th Century American Quotations* (New York: A Stonesong Press Book, 1992) 269.

The Parable of Wait Till Next Year

Theophilus said, "When a team has a bad season, the coach, members of the team, and fans say, 'Wait till next year.'"

Jeremiah saw things going from bad to worse, so he turned to the Lord for encouragement. The Lord said, "Jeremiah, if you get tired of racing against men, how can you race against horses?"[19]

Strangely enough, although Jeremiah's life became more difficult, by learning to run with men he soon could keep up with the horses.

One of the great hopes of sports fans is that their team will be able to turn their season around. The personnel is good, so all we have to do is turn it around.

The losers occasionally rise to a great effort to pull off an amazing upset. Then the next week they are beaten, because having beaten a horse they are unequal to the more demanding task of running with men.

The same pattern follows in most people's lives. Our junior high record wasn't good, but wait till high school, that record wasn't good but wait till college. We know that we have the talent and all we have to do is put forth the effort. Then why don't we do well? It is because we think we don't have to compete with men since we think we are the horses; at the same time the winners are working harder to get where they are.

Proverbs 27:1 – Never boast about tomorrow. You don't know what will happen between now and then.

---

[19] Jeremiah 12:5.

RACING

*"Run the straight race through God's good grace,
lift up thine eyes and seek his face;
life with its way before us lies,
Christ is the path and Christ the prize."*

❋

John Samuel Bewley Monsell
(1811 - 1875)

The Parable of Fixing A Race

An article once said, "An attempt to influence a rider into fixing the outcome of a horse race won't come from a stranger in a trench coat who looks like he just stepped out of a Humphrey Bogart movie. It is more likely to come from someone you know."[1]

I would suspect that many Christians do not understand what they are praying when they say, "Lead us not into temptation," because surely this is not what "Our Father" would do. However, in New Testament usage to tempt a person is not so much to seek to seduce him into sin as it is to test his strength and his loyalty and his ability to serve.[2]

Whether temptation means a bad word or a testing, the same warnings apply. The first piece of advice is: "It does not matter how small the sins are provided that their cumulative effect is to edge the man away from the light and out into the Nothing. Murder is no better than cards if cards can do the trick. Indeed the safest road to Hell is the gradual one - the gentle slope."[3] And the most profound warning is, "The last temptation is the greatest treason. To do the right thing for the wrong reason."[4]

Matthew 6:13 - Do not bring us to hard testing, but keep us safe from the Evil One.

---

[1] *Sports Illustrated*, 8 December 1975.

[2] William Barclay, *The Gospel of Matthew* (Philadelphia: The Westminster Press, 1975), 224.

[3] C. S. Lewis, *The Screwtape Letters* (New York: The MacMillan Company, 1952), 64.

[4] T. S. Eliot, *Murder in the Cathedral* (A Harvest Book, Harcourt, Brace and World, Inc., 1963), 44.

The Parable of the Pits

During the running of an important five hundred mile automobile race, there was a commercial on TV which said, "You can't win on the track if you don't win in the pits." The pit crew is trained to get their race car back on the track as soon as possible - re-gassing, re-tooling, re-tiring. They wave the driver back on the track. You can't win sitting in the pit.

Sooner or later, each one of us will have to make a pit stop. Our free-wheeling days are broken by a tragedy, by ill health, by a family dispute. Any number of breakdowns can put us in the pits. The pit crew is trained in its split-second regimen to get the driver and his powerful machine back on the track. Some of us are tempted to make the pit our home. We settle down there and rather enjoy not being involved in the race. It is more comfortable and certainly less dangerous.

The great souls have had their powers called out by the very problems they face. A person needs a competitive spirit if he is to get rolling again. Who has not seen and known those among us who have become new spirits by their pit experience?

If you are in the pits you have the ability to get back on track.

Romans 12:21 - Do not let evil defeat you; instead, conquer evil with good.

The Parable of an Eight Year Old

A certain owner entered an eight year old non-starter in his first race. Needless to say, an eight year old maiden was not a betting favorite. He went off at $136.50 and came in first by ten lengths. The steward suspected dirty work and asked, "Is this horse unsound?" The owner said, "No, sir, soundest horse you ever saw." "Well, then," the steward asked, "Why haven't you raced him before?" The owner said, "To tell you the truth, we couldn't catch him till he was seven."[5]

The dominion of man over animals begins in the Garden of Eden and continues in religious writings. Growing up, in cowboy movies there was often the story of the great stallion that both the good and the bad guys were trying to catch.

In our parable, this horse took seven years to catch. But once they controlled its mouth, they controlled the horse. So, if people "can control the tongue we can control the whole body, but if the tongue is uncontrolled the whole life is set on the wrong way."[6]

"So it is with the tongue: small as it is, it can boast about great things."[7]

James 3:3 - We put a bit into the mouth of a horse to make it obey us, and we are able to make it go where we want.

---

[5] Bennet Cerf, *Bennet Cerf's Bumper Crop, Vol. 1* (Garden City, NY: Garden City Books, 1959), 269.
[6] William Barclay, *The Letters of James and Peter* (Philadelphia: The Westminster Press, 1975), 84.
[7] James 3:5.

The Parable of A Goat

Theophilus said, "Racing men often place a goat in the stall with a nervous race horse. The horse soon becomes accustomed to having a goat in there and finds it very comforting; he becomes less nervous and is not so easily upset. If, however, the owner of a rival horse can steal or 'get' the goat then the horse is even more nervous than before and may lose the race."[8]

The race horse finds comfort from the presence of a goat, and he experiences anxiety when the goat disappears.

When someone gets your goat you also need a comforter. A baby may need the comfort of a pacifier. On a cold night, we use a comforter. In John's gospel, the Holy Spirit is called the comforter - which means helper. So a comforter is a helper.

Between II Corinthians 1:3-9 the noun "comfort" and the verb "to comfort" are found nine times in many translations of the New Testament.

Comfort comes from the Latin *fortis - brave*. Christian comfort brings courage and enables a man to face all that life can do to him.

The comfort of a goat can enable a horse to run the race. The comfort of God enables us to do the same.

Isaiah 40:1 – "Comfort my people," says our God. "Comfort them!"

---

[8] *Why Do We Say It?* (Edison, NJ: Castle Book, 1985), 105.

The Parable of the Leader

Theophilus and his friends were watching a marathon. As the leader of the field approached he said, "In a marathon the leader runs alone."

One of the more difficult things to do in life is to take a position which is away from the pack. We are so much more comfortable being surrounded by others who keep the same pace that we do.

The chief characteristics of a distance runner are:

- He knows what pace he is capable of maintaining

- He has the courage to take the lead because he has faith that he can reach his goal.

- He doesn't need to look back to see if others are following.

A leader is a person who knows any goal will require time and determination. To accomplish his mission a leader does not wait to see how the wind is blowing; he is willing to take his position in front. A leader has the freedom to fail if he is beaten at the finish.

Most important issues are in the long run not a sprint but a matter of endurance.

I Corinthians 9:24b – Run, then, in such a way as to win the prize.

The Parable of the High Bar

He was not a star athlete. He was tall and skinny, so the coach told him that he was too slow for track and he should try to jump in the field events. He never won an event. but in the pole vault and the high-jump he got enough points to help his team win district. He never got to go to the regional or state meets.

A jumper doesn't know how high he can jump until he fails to clear the bar. Success is reaching your potential. "The people who are really failures are the people who set their standards so low, keep the bar at such a safe level, that they don't run the risk."[9]

The greatest of all freedoms is the freedom to fail. Americans love a winner. Americans support winners with attendance and adoration. Christians realize that we need love the most when we fail. A Christian parent should never break off a relationship with a child regardless of what he or she does. This is the message of God from the Cross - "Forgive them, Father! They don't know what they are doing."[10]

Matthew 6:12 - Forgive us the wrongs we have done, as we forgive the wrongs that others have done to us.

---

[9] Robert H. Schuler, *Tough Minded Faith for Tender Hearted People* (Nashville: Thomas Nelson Publishers, 1982), 10.
[10] Luke 23:34.

The Parable of the Man Against the Horse

A certain track star[11] received $2,000 for outrunning a horse in a 100 yard dash. Later he said, "Of course, there is no way a man can really beat a horse, even over 100 yards. The secret is, first, get a thoroughbred because they are the most nervous animals on earth. Then, get the biggest gun you can and make sure the starter fires that big gun right by the nervous thoroughbred's ear. By the time the jockey gets his horse settled down, I could run about 50 yards."[12]

That track star said, "I had four gold medals, but you can't eat four gold medals." He was able to run this race because of his fame. He, like the unjust steward, took advantage of his position and should be commended for his shrewdness, not because he did right.

I've seen people begin their Christian pilgrimage to please their wife, others for business reasons, others for the purpose of getting something to eat. Judas thought Jesus would help lead the revolution against Roman rule. Most of the other eleven apostles didn't understand Jesus' teachings. Peter, after his faith confession, betrayed. The message of scripture is clear. God takes what we bring, good and bad, and converts it to his purpose.

I Corinthians 15:9b-10a - I do not even deserve to be called an apostle, because I persecuted God's church. But by God's grace, I am what I am.

---

[11] Jesse Owens.

[12] William Oscar Johnson, *The Olympics – A History of the Games* (Oxmoor House, 1993), 71.

The Parable of the First Day

A certain Olympic runner[13] was hopeful of winning a spot on the upcoming Olympic team. At the trials he failed to qualify. He was interviewed and asked, "What do you plan to do now?" He replied, "Tomorrow is the first day of the rest of my life."[14]

Our competitive athletic years are short. If this is all we live for then the next day often ends in unhappiness. Our talents are wasted if used only for worldly glory that fades away.

"If you do not believe in another, higher world, if you believe only in the flat material world around you, if you believe this is your only chance for happiness - if that is what you believe, then you are more than disappointed when the world does not give you a good measure of its riches, you are in despair."[15]

Christians believe in two worlds. After we have finished the course then we have another world to look forward to. Death is not the end but the first day of the rest of our life.

Romans 8:18 – I consider that what we suffer at the present time cannot be compared at all with the glory that is going to be revealed to us.

---

[13] Billy Mills.
[14] *Sports Illustrated*, September 23, 1968, 19.
[15] Peggy Noonan, *Life, Liberty and the Pursuit of Happiness* (New York: Random House, 1994), 214-215.

The Parable of Charismata

"The long, long homestretch of Belmont Park is known as the graveyard of champions. It is littered with the broken dreams and the bleached bones of Triple Crown contenders, and somewhere along its dusty avenue on Saturday, a racehorse named Charismatic snapped bones in his left leg."[16]

Unlike humans, a broken leg is a life and death issue for horses. The love that caused the jockey[17] to jump off the horse and hold up his leg from likely fatal damage is charismata (a gift of grace).

In life there are many charismatic acts; they occur most often when a person thinks only of the welfare of the other. The newspapers are full of stories of a person risking his/her own life to save another. There are also the attempts that are made to hold someone up in a crisis moment to try to avoid further damage, the support we receive in the many agonies of defeat.

The message of this parable is not the jockey or the horse, not the helper or the helped, but the charismata given to Charismatic.

I Corinthians 14:3 – But the one who proclaims God's message speaks to people and gives them help, encouragement and comfort.

---

[16] Billy Lyon, *Knight Ridder Newspaper* (Corpus Christi Caller Times, June 7, 1999), C-4.
[17] Chris Antley.

SOCCER
&
HOCKEY

*"The tension is so bad.
You know if you make a mistake
it's not just your club you're hurting,
you're hurting the whole nation."*

Nobby Stiles, English soccer player,
on World Cup Tournament

A Parable on Simplicity

Theophilus said, "The great thing about soccer is that there are very few rules, they are easy to understand. It requires no expensive equipment. This is why it is the most popular sport in the world."

In America, simplicity is not a virtue. We are a land of "How are you doing?" rather than "How are you?" Doing is more important than being.

Before I retired I asked a friend "What is the biggest problem with retirement except the economic change?" He said "It is only a problem for those who get their identity from what they do, rather than who they are."

People's attitude toward soccer reminds me of retirement, people look at it and yell "boring." It is because they can't see the beauty in simplicity.

Philippians 4:11b – ". . . I have learned to be satisfied with what I have."

The Parable of Pre-Match Ritual

A certain soccer captain said, "I always put my left pad on first. I always hang my towel on my peg with my clothes, not on the bench like the other lads. When I lead the lads out, I always bounce the ball twice on the ceiling in the corridor."[1]

When players are preparing for a game, there are many who follow the same order, ritual and ceremony each time. The order is when each thing is done, the ritual is the left pad and the towel peg, the ceremony is the ball twice on the ceiling. Does it affect the outcome? Likely not, but it helps this player to get ready for the action.

In churches, an order of worship is usually handed out, the ritual is what everyone does and says, and the ceremony is how it is done. Every church has its own ritual, and this is why it is so difficult to visit another church. We don't know what to do even with a program.

When a person follows the ritual and ceremony often enough, it becomes part of a routine. It means that we are prepared to participate.

In sports and worship, some form of private ritual helps us to get ready for our ritual with others.

I Peter 3:15 - But have reverence for Christ in your hearts, and honor him as Lord. Be ready at all times to answer anyone who asks you to explain the hope you have in you.

---

[1] Hunter Davies, *The Glory Game* (Edinburgh, Scotland: Mainstream Publishing, 1985), 310.

The Parable of Angles

A certain boy, who was tall, lean and agile, was trying to learn how to play goalie for his soccer team. The coach was kicking balls at him from all different positions on the field. He learned he didn't have to protect the whole goal, he only had to cover the different angles.

When problems seem to be coming at us from all directions, it is important to learn from the goalie to cut down the angles.

This is, of course, the problem of the old adage of not being able to see the trees for the forest. With a multitude of shots coming at us, it's important to know how to respond by knowing where the problem is.

We see so many difficulties we are unable to deal with the one at hand. A loving response when we are being attacked can protect our goal. We don't have to deal with everything but only the immediate. If we learn how to handle the immediate we can learn not to be overwhelmed by the different situations that we face which come from all directions.

I Peter 4:8 - Above everything, love one another earnestly, because love covers over many sins.

Parable of a National Team

When soccer's top female[2] flew back from China in 1991, the lady sitting next to her on the plane asked where she had been. She explained that she had just played in the world championship soccer tournament. "How'd you do?" the woman asked. "We won." "That's nice," the woman said.[3]

Almost anyone who reads this page will have to go to the footnotes to know the name of the person in footnote 2, or that the United States won the inaugural Women's World Cup.

In our daily lives, when something great happens we often say, "That's nice." If something bad occurs, then we respond with some kind of compassion or outrage, but it is a response. The worst response is when we do something well and no one cares.

When we appreciate what someone has done and tell them, then "that's nice."

Proverbs 31:27-28 – She is always busy and looks after her family's needs. Her children show their appreciation, and her husband praises her.

---

[2] Michelle Akers Stah.

[3] Kelly Whiteside, *Sports Illustrated*, June 5, 1995, Vol. 8, pg. 72.

The Parable of the Big Goal

Theophilus gave this parable: "The main problem with being a goalie is that the goal is too big."

In the game of soccer, the goal that must be defended by a goalie is 24 feet across and 8 feet high. It is rather obvious that it is basically indefensible.

As witnesses to Christ, we also find that our goal is too big. Most of us are in the position of the goalie. We are defenders of the faith, but our responsibility is beyond our reach. We are called to stop another kind of puck (a class of evil spirits) so the question is, "How can we position ourselves against offensive beliefs about the Christian faith?"

I found myself in this defensive position until I read this admonition: "Knowing ourselves as sinners, we need never tone down our witness to what we have already achieved, nor need we have a bad conscience about preaching what we do not yet practice. Knowing this we are free to proclaim, with joy and gratitude, what we do not yet practice, and in doing so we are effectively called into repentance."[4]

Romans 10:14b - And how can they hear if the message is not proclaimed?

---

[4] Werner Pelz, *Religious Reflections on the Christian Church* (Naperville, IL: SCM Book Club, 1985), 30.

The Parable of Absolute Joy

A mother took her child to see a stage production of *Snow White and the Seven Dwarfs*. The announcement came from a manager on the stage - U.S.A. 4, Finland 2. The United States had just won the gold in ice hockey. The place erupted, the audience rose to their feet cheering, they began singing the Star Spangled Banner and the orchestra joined in. It was two or three minutes of absolute joy![5]

I can't remember when I didn't feel the good news of God in Christ. It has always been good, but seldom news. It is very difficult to find joy in the expected. It is easy to find satisfaction, but not joy. We need to be surprised by joy to feel the exhilaration. "I once was lost but now am found" is an expression of amazing grace. The problem comes for those who always knew where they were and whose they were.

I once heard Gert Behanna tell her story of despair turning to joy. She gave credit to the faithful who kept the church doors open for her to return. It is awfully easy to develop the elder brother's attitude instead of knowing the joy of welcoming the unexpected.

Luke 17:10b – . . . when you have done all you have been told to do, say, "We are ordinary servants; we have only done our duty."

---

[5] Dudley Clendine, New York Times, February 25, 1980, Section C, page 1.

The Parable of No Stats

A man said to his friend, "I like soccer, an elegant dance of skill and endurance, and am utterly baffled by the appeal of American football, which consists of spasms of extreme violence devoid of grace and nuance . . . What's the problem with soccer?" "No stats," my friend Bud explained. "Americans don't like sports. They like stats."[6]

This seemed like a silly answer until I realized that so many millions of us play Fantasy Sports Games. These games are all based on statistics, which soccer doesn't have.

I also recall a home run that my wife and I saw that would have been just another defeat for our Washington Senators. However, it was a record 565 foot home run hit by Mickey Mantle. What made it memorable? The stats!

Statistics help your anamnesis, but another statistic tells the story. In the 1994 World Cup, "In the 206 games played in the qualifying round, 120 were shutouts, including 20 scoreless ties."[7] This leads to amnesia.

Malachi 3:16b – In his presence, there was written down in a book a record of those who feared the Lord and respected Him.

---

[6] Robert L. Welsh, (Natural History, January, 1995), 16.
[7] Ibid., 17.

TENNIS
&
VOLLEYBALL

"When I was forty, my doctor advised me that a man in his forties shouldn't play tennis.
I heeded his advice carefully and could hardly wait until I reached fifty to start again."

Justice Hugo Black,
the United States Supreme Court

The Parable of the Love Game

A group of young people went to their first tennis camp. The instructor began with a lecture on the history of tennis. When he was finished, he asked if there were any questions. A student asked, "When I don't score any points, why do we call it a love game?"

A famous sportswriter once wrote:

Write this above my dust in some lost grave,
"Here lies no hero, listed with the brave,
He had no thought of glory or of fame
Beyond the score, he only loved the game.
And when the bell gave out its ringing call
He had not much to give but gave it all."[1]

A person who plays because he loves the game is called an amateur, which comes from the Latin *amare* (to love). An amateur means playing for nothing, and this is why having no score is called "love".

Some play the Christian game for what they can get out of it, and even look for a victory in a game.

"An amateur Christian is not concerned with rewards. Christian love is returning God's love. This is the love game."[2]

John 15:12 - My commandment is this: love one another, just as I love you.

---

[1] Grantland Rice, *The Final Answer and Other Poems* (New York: A. S. Barnes and Co., 1995), 66.
[2] Charles H. Long, ed., *Forward Day By Day* (Cincinnati: Forward Movement Publications, 1994), Vol. 59, No. 4, 88.

The Parable of the Linesman

This is a parable for those who have to make quick decisions: A certain linesman was instructing a new linesman on the important rules of conduct.   The most important is that "out" and "fault" calls should be made immediately after the ball hits the court, with a loud and clear voice.   There is no call if the ball is in bounds.   If you make a bad call you can say "correction" and give the right call.[3]

Although I've never been a linesman, it would seem to me that it's better to make no call than to say it was out, which stops play.   It is easier to correct an "in" that was "out", than an "out" that was "in."

When my daughter was a teenager she asked, "Daddy, why do you always say no when I ask if I can do something?"   I replied, "Because you never ask me any questions with yes answers."   Can I go to church is not asked, the question is can I go to the beach.

As a general rule it is best, when you have to decide immediately, to say "No."   This is because "no" can easily be corrected to "yes", but there is great tribulation if "yes" is turned into a "no."   A "no" also produces information that serves as a better basis for a decision.

If you feel that in your prayers God is always saying "no", you should try some prayers with "yes" answers.

James 5:12b - Say only "Yes" when you mean yes, and "No" when you mean no.

---

[3] Roy Wilder, *Friends of Tennis* (Lynn, MA: H. O. Zimmerman Inc., 1962), 153, adapted.

The Parable of Serving

Theophilus said to his friend, "I've got a test for you." The friend said, "What's that?" Theophilus said, "In what sport can you only win when you are serving?"

As a friend of Theophilus, I have played or watched many sports. However, the only sport I could think of as an answer was volleyball. Theophilus said, "That's the one I had in mind. When you are not serving you can only win the service back."

In Webster's New International Unabridged Dictionary, there are 33 definitions of "serve". They range from a waiter to a public servant.

In Jesus' day, the most used title for a king was benefactor. Jesus tells his apostles that in his kingdom those who serve are benefactors. Humility replaces glory, and service replaces rule.

In volleyball, the only way to make a point is by serving. In the Christian life, the point is serving.

Luke 22:27 - Who is greater, the one who sits down to eat or the one who serves him? The one who sits down, of course. But I am among you as one who serves.

The Parable of a Tournament

The National Intercollegiate Tennis Tournament was held in a certain town. The winds were awful, the coaches asked that the next tournament be moved to another city, and it appeared the tournament would be moved. However, the NCAA committee returned it to the same city. The tournament director[4] said that God returned the tournament to this city and would give us good weather.[5]

It is very disappointing to see bad theology on a sports page or on a TV interview. When I hear an athlete thank God for the victory of his team I wonder if he also believes that God caused the loss for the other team and had something against the other town. In this case, two years later God must have liked them better than us, because the tournament was moved to the other town.

I see and hear too many people looking for God to intervene and pull out a plum, a prize, a victory, or a miracle for their lives. They do not do the necessary work, planning, and effort which produce miracles. Behind every miracle there is a great deal of human effort.

I have seen Christians produce many miracles, but I haven't seen miracles produce many Christians.

Matthew 5:45b - For he makes his sun to shine on bad and good people alike, and gives rain to those who do good and to those who do evil.

---

[4] Bob Mapes.
[5] Corpus Christi Caller Times, 8 May 1976.

The Parable of Sight and Sound

There was a girl[6] who was blind since the age of four. She began playing tennis when she was a sixteen year old high school junior. At first she spent several hours a day practicing against a backboard using special balls implanted with tiny bells. By concentrating on the sound of the object she couldn't see, she reached the point where she felt she was ready for actual competition; she soon began to hold her own against sighted friends.[7]

After a year of playing with the "tinkle balls," she began playing with regular balls. She was able to play a creditable game by focusing on the sound of the ball.

"Keep your eye on the ball" is the most common advice in all sports that use a ball. Equally important is concentration on the action and the results to be achieved.

Trying to "see" the Christian faith, we can see what is written, but we also have to know where it is coming from. Anything written about our faith depends as much on what you hear as what the author wrote. The Christian faith has so many types of expression that some Christians only want to hear what they already see. We prefer to remain in the dark to the fact that Christianity is like love, a many splendored thing. Listening in tennis helps you know the spin on the ball. Listening in Christianity helps us understand the different spins on our faith.

I Corinthians 12:7 - The Spirit's presence is shown in some way in each person for the good of all.

---

[6] Chris Ehlor.

[7] Billie Jean King and Greg Hoffman, *Tennis Love* (New York: MacMillan Publishing Co., 1978), 126.

The Parable of a Name

Theophilus said, "There were two tennis partners[8] who had played only on the Atlantic coastline. They decided to go to California to play. One came back enthused and said, 'The West has an enormous potential for the development of tennis and a large international competition would help tennis grow in popularity.' He requested 217 ounces of silver from a Boston silversmith, and a cup was made and called the International Lawn Challenge Cup. As is the case with most names that are too long, it was soon changed to the Davis Cup."[9]

Most things are too long. Have you ever heard anyone complain about a sermon being too short? What is remembered in a great speech is the one line.

In all the years I've read about, listened to, or watched the Davis Cup tournament, it never occurred to me to wonder who Davis was. Most of us want to make a difference, to contribute something of lasting value, but we'd be hard put to name anything we've done that is really important.

Dwight Davis contributed mightily to international tennis. His name lives but not the reason. What difference have you made? It is usually one little deed that affected many people, and they didn't even know your name.

Ecclesiastes. 2:16 - No one remembers wise men, and no one remembers fools. In days to come, we will all be forgotten.

---

[8] Dwight Davis and Holcombe Ward.
[9] Gianmi Clerk, *The Ultimate Tennis Book* (Chicago: Follett Publishing Co., 1975) 83.

The Parable of a Game Plan

A promising junior player took in everything he was taught by his teaching pro, but in close matches he lacked confidence. The pro suggested his player work out his own game plan. It worked! His plan to rush the net on both his serves was not succeeding. He was being passed by his opponent's backhand cross-court. When he changed his game plan he closed out the match by holding his serve and cashing in two service breaks.[10]

The coach has done his job, his student has grown to the point where he can make his own decisions. However, the pupil remains a pupil and the coach continues to help develop his skills by suggestions on how to improve. Match by match he must rise to a higher level.

God has done his job. He has made us members of his family. As children by adoption we didn't earn being children. He is head of the family, we respond to his love with gratitude. Our goodness is a response. As we practice our faith, we don't do good things to get in God's good graces; our response comes from his graces that motivate us to be good.

Philippians 2:12 - So then, dear friends, as you always obeyed me when I was with you, it is even more important that you obey me now while I am away from you. Keep on working with fear and trembling to complete your salvation.

---

[10] M. Barrie Richmond, *Total Tennis* (New York: MacMillan Publishing Co., 1980), 120.

AMEN

*"I don't wish to sound pretentious in any way,
but I've always tried to teach by using stories or parables.
I figure if it was good enough for the Bible,
it's good enough for Harvey Penick."*

❧

Harvey Penick – University of Texas
golf coach for 32 years

The Parable of Amen Corner

A sportswriter[1] describing Amen Corner said, "It looks like something that fell from heaven, but it plays like something straight out of hell."[2]

Amen Corner (the second half of the 11th hole, the short 12th, and the first half of the 13th at the Augusta National Golf Coarse in Augusta, Georgia) was named by Warren Wind in a 1957 article for *Sports Illustrated*. He borrowed the name from an old jazz recording, "Shouting at Amen Corner."[3] His expression caught on, perhaps because a golfer, Dave Marr, suggested, "If you get through these three holes in even par you believe a bit more in God."[4]

For me the parable is about writing a book. The idea comes to you and you feel like it came as direct inspiration from Heaven. You complete your masterpiece and send it to numerous publishers, and it plays like something out of Hell.

If you are reading these words say "Amen" because we made it through, and I hope you believe a bit more in God. Amen.

Revelation 22:20b-21 – Amen. Even so, come, Lord Jesus. The grace of our Lord Jesus Christ be with you all. Amen. King James Version

---

[1] Gary Van Sickle.
[2] Milwaukee Journal, 1981.
[3] George Pepper, *Grand Slam Golf* (New York: Harry N. Abrams, 1991), 21.
[4] Ibid.

DIVISION QUOTATIONS

BASEBALL - Lee Green, *Sportswit* (New York: Harper and Row Publishers, 1984), 28.

BASKETBALL - Andrew J. Maikovich, ed., *Sports Quotations* (Jefferson, NC: McFarland and Co., 1984), 56.

BOXING - Andrew J. Maikovich, ed., *Sports Quotations* (Jefferson, NC: McFarland and Co., 1984), 59.

FOOTBALL - Andrew J. Maikovich, ed., *Sports Quotations* (Jefferson, NC: McFarland and Co., 1984), 89.

GOLF - Lee Green, *Sportswit* (New York: Harper and Row Publishers, 1984), 149.

HUNTING, FISHING & SAILING - Edmund Fuller, ed., *2500 Anecdotes for All Occasions* (New York: Avenal Books, 1978), 332.

MOST SPORTS - Lee Green, *Sportswit* (New York: Harper and Row Publishers, 1984), 194.

RACING - *The Hymnal 1982* (New York: The Church Hymnal Corporation, 1985), Hymn 552.

SOCCER & HOCKEY - Andrew J. Maikovich, ed., *Sports Quotations* (Jefferson, NC: McFarland and Co., 1984), 1695.

TENNIS & VOLLEYBALL - Laurence J. Peter, *Peter's Quotations* (New York: William Morrow and Company, 1977), 452.

AMEN - Don Wade, *"And Then Jack Said To Arnie . . ."* (Lincolnwood, IL: Contemporary Books, 1991), 146.